Books by Parke Rouse:

The City That Turned Back Time

Virginia: the English Heritage in America

Below the James Lies Dixie: Smithfield and Southside, Virginia

Planters and Pioneers: Life in Colonial Virginia

Endless Harbor: the Story of Newport News

James Blair of Virginia

The Great Wagon Road: from Philadelphia to the South

Cows on the Campus: Williamsburg in Bygone Days

Virginia: A Pictorial History

When Williamsburg Woke Up:
Dr. Goodwin, Mr. Rockefeller, and the Restoration

A House for a President:
250 Years on the Campus of the College of William and Mary

Living by Design: Leslie Cheek and the Arts

The Good Old Days in Hampton and Newport News

The Timber Tycoons: The Camp Families of Virginia and Florida

Remembering Williamsburg:
A Sentimental Journey through Three Centuries

The James: Where a Nation Began

Along Virginia's Golden Shores: Glimpses of Tidewater Life

George Washington: Patron of Learning and Father of Philanthropy
at Washington and Lee University

We Happy WASPs: Virginia in the Days of Jim Crow and Harry Byrd

Jamestown's Story: Act One of the American Dream

Hampton In the Bygone Days

AFTER THE GUNBOATS LANDED

AFTER THE GUNBOATS LANDED

Civil War and Reconstruction
on the Virginia Peninsula

A Memoir
by George Benjamin West

Edited by Parke S. Rouse, Jr.

Designed by
Marshall Rouse McClure

PARKE PRESS
Norfolk, Virginia
www.parkepress.com

ISBN 978-0-9843339-4-3

Library of Congress Control Number is available upon request

Printed in the United States of America

To Dorothy Rouse-Bottom,
who encouraged me to make this story available
anew to students of American history.

TABLE OF CONTENTS

HISTORIANS CAN EXAMINE events of the past and, usually, place them within the context of broader life-changing experiences. This can happen in almost any situation, but wartime offers the opportunity to scrutinize not only the military effects upon a region, but also the societal interactions and longtime influences that warfare is catalyst to.

Nothing, however, makes as strong a mark, nor gives rise to as careful an examination of events, as those observations of individuals in the middle of history being made every day.

Diaries, journals and memoirs written during or shortly after significant historical events can add depth and breadth to any eventual scholarly examination. Unfortunately, through the years, few such personal narratives have survived and when they do, the accounts often are found to be trivial in nature, more like family dinner table conversations than observations of significant occasions.

In 2010, the University of Virginia Press published, for The Mariners' Museum of Newport News, Virginia, the journals of George Randolph Wood. Entitled *A Young Virginia Boatman Navigates The Civil War*, this is an account from early 1861 until April 1865 during Wood's brief time as a prisoner. The volume has been critically acclaimed for its contribution to subjects previously unexplored.

Similarly, in 2000, the Virginia Historical Society arranged for the publication of *Eye of the Storm*, written and illustrated by Private Robert Knox Sneden, a Union soldier, whose words and pictures take the reader into the front assault lines of the Civil War. This accounting was especially praised for its depiction of a soldier's life during that war.

After the Gunboats Landed, this memoir of George Benjamin West, edited by Parke Rouse, Jr. and originally published in 1977, is on equal footing: it, too, covers unexplored facets of the Civil War. These memoirs describe, in a flowing narrative, domestic life on Virginia's Peninsula during the Union occupation, and the West family's flight to a safer Richmond, away from the Union-held territory. Equally compelling are accounts of the ruined Peninsula after the war, and the plight of area citizens during Reconstruction.

Like the Virginia boatman Wood, West wrote his observations after the fact, and his memoir permits the reader to weave together the lives of the many landsmen who lived near Newport News Point, where several generations of West's family tilled the soil. West himself was no farmer, but he understood their plight and became a leading citizen of the area after the war, as the town of Newport News grew into a small city.

In 2012, the sesquicentennial observance of the American Civil War is underway and it seems fitting to reintroduce this memorable account of another young person's look at warfare and its aftermath. For most Virginia Peninsula residents, the Federal troops were invaders whose presence changed the status quo in ways important and trivial. Parke Rouse, in his editorial notations, places West's narrative in the larger context of the modern-day Peninsula. He points out historical references and personalities to help readers understand those vast changes that began in Virginia after the gunboats landed.

– Wilford Kale
Williamsburg, 2012

A Man of Two Worlds

WHEN VIRGINIA VOTED ON APRIL 17, 1861 TO secede from the union, it doomed itself to become the battleground of the war between North and South. It had not long to wait. Six weeks later, farmers living at Newport News Point, at the juncture of Hampton Roads and the James River, saw troop-laden vessels approaching their shore. The Yankees had come! The feared invasion of the Peninsula was at hand. The Federal assault on the Confederate capital at Richmond was about to take shape.

One of the few onlookers at Newport News that fateful morning—May 27, 1861—was a pudgy lad of 22 whose family owned a farm and dock on the James. He was George Benjamin West, whose idyllic youth ended forever that day. Thinking back later of that placid Sunday before the Yankees came, George Ben West wrote: "This was the last happy day spent in our pleasant home, and how happy we were in the enjoyment

George Benjamin West wrote his memoirs in his 60s, at the close of the nineteenth century. For years his portrait hung in the Newport News bank he founded.

One of the buildings of Parker West's farm can be seen in this view of Newport News Point by Edward Bruce in **Harper's New Monthly Magazine** *in 1859.*

of the present. . . ." Ahead lay his family's hasty flight up the Peninsula, four years of refugee life in Richmond and Lynchburg, and finally the survivors' return to Newport News in 1865, to find a desolated farm and a changed world.

George West's memoirs, which he wrote thirty years after the war, are a graphic account of turbulent years—a minuscule *Gone With the Wind* of suffering buoyed up by hope. But there was to be a happy ending. Newport News grew into a town in 1880, after Collis Potter Huntington made it the terminus of his Chesapeake and Ohio Railway, and George West became a prosperous leading citizen, living comfortably until he died at 78 in 1917. By that time, Newport News was again about to be engulfed in war—this time of global scope.

The 22-year-old West was living in 1861 with his parents, Parker and Mary West, in a wooden farmhouse which fronted the James near what would be Eleventh Street, now occupied by the coal-handling piers of the Chesapeake and Ohio Railway. He was the sixth of seven children, several of whom died in childhood.

George Ben West never married, and only two of his sisters did so.

Intensely devoted to his family, he took to live with him in the large Victorian house he built at Thirty-fourth Street and West Avenue, his youngest sister, Missouri West Smith, who had left her husband, and Mrs. Smith's daughter, Emily. After Emily in 1892 married William E. Barrett, an attorney and realtor, she and her husband became a part of her doting "Uncle Boo's" household.

Newport News Point was in 1861 a verdant farm peninsula, with only Parker West's farmhouse and a few other structures among its fields and woods. The 303-acre Parker West farm stood on a bluff with a grove of cedars between it and the river. Near the western end of his farm, about where Eighteenth Street now runs, Parker West in 1860 built a wharf, which was depicted in a *Harper's Weekly* drawing of Newport News' waterfront in 1861. Nearby was a freshwater spring which had been used by ships since John Smith's time and a wharf built in 1851 by R. E. Bennett, who had established the vicinity's first tiny post-office there on October 15, 1851. Here passengers and farm produce for Richmond or Norfolk were picked up by river steamers.

Ships entering the James River had stopped at this point from the time of John Smith, in 1607, for a freshwater spring flowed from the earth near the present Eighteenth Street, where Parker West in 1860 built his dock and a two-storied warehouse. The deep water and the semi-protected harbor led West to believe Newport News would become a major port, as he often told his family. A New England peddler, Collis P. Huntington, debarked at Newport News Point in the 1830s and also thought it an ideal site for a port, he said later.

In bad weather, dozens of river schooners sought haven along the waterfront of the Wests' and adjoining farmers. "In long easterly spells there were often a hundred or more at anchor," George Ben West recalled in 1911. These two- and three-masted vessels loaded cordwood cut near Newport News, plus corn, oats, wheat, and especially sweet potatoes. Schooner captains bought Newport News' prized sweet potatoes, and steamships stopped there at Bennett's wharf to load them and other perishables. Nearly every Newport News area farmer had an orchard—many households made their own apple and peach brandy —and plums, apricots, cherries, peaches, pears, and apples were sent to Norfolk to market, together with peas, beans, cabbage, and melons. Tobacco, a crop once widely grown on the Peninsula, had by

1800 moved largely to the warmer "black belt" counties south of the James River.

Farm clearings on the lower Peninsula were modest in size and were separated by pine forests. Narrow dirt roads linked the various plantations with Hampton, the region's commercial center, and with Yorktown and Williamsburg.

In 1861 the Newport News area farms were so few that George Ben West could recall them accurately fifty years later. In a talk to the Pioneers' Club of Newport News in 1911, he listed holders of every property from the present Sixty-seventh Street in Newport News to the present LaSalle Avenue in Hampton, following the shore of the lower Peninsula from the lower James into Hampton Roads. These acreages ranged from 109 to 333—modest by 1860 Virginia standards—and were nearly all farmed by the owner and several black field hands, as in the case of Parker West. A few landowners lived elsewhere and rented out their Newport News property, or depended on overseers to farm it.

Union sailors alongside James River bank in a landing craft.

Parker West and a few other well-to-do farmers owned houses in Hampton and went to that Elizabeth City County seat on "court days" for medical attention, or during school terms to permit their children to enroll. Some Newport News area farmers often spent the winter in Hampton, during the quiet season on the farm—just as James River planters in colonial times had moved to Williamsburg for Public Times each year.

Of his early neighbors George Ben West wrote:

> None of them were rich, but all were well-to-do, owned their farms, and had sufficient slaves for household and farm work. . . . The slaves were notably well-treated, well-fed, and well-housed; they were seldom bought or sold. They married either their masters' slaves or those of their neighbors. They attended and belonged to the churches of their owners. . . . Not a single one left his master, though they had every opportunity to do so in the vessels that traded up the James River.

Parker West and his wife, Mary Drummond Bell West, had come to Newport News Point from the Eastern Shore of Virginia in 1831, first buying a Newport News farm and thereafter acquiring other farms and some two dozen rental houses in Hampton. Newport News Point then was part of Elizabeth City County, the line dividing it from tiny Warwick County running roughly down the center of the lower Peninsula to a point near the present Forty-fourth Street and Marshall Avenue, then veering southwesterly to reach the James River at approximately the present Eighteenth Street in Newport News. After the Chesapeake and Ohio Railway was built in 1882, the Warwick-Elizabeth City line was straightened to place Newport News Point in Warwick County. In 1896 the General Assembly declared Newport News an independent city. In 1958, Warwick County was merged with Newport News just as Elizabeth City County had merged with Hampton six years earlier.

In 1844 Parker and Mary West moved their family temporarily from Newport News to Hampton to enable their children to attend school. There six-year-old George West entered John B. Cary's military academy, acquiring a foundation of language, mathematics, and other subjects which enabled him to enter the University of Virginia in 1860, aged 20. A shy and self-conscious lad, he never

A Jamestown 250th celebration encampment, 1857.

enjoyed the verbal recitations, punctilio, and punishments of military school. At the time, he confessed later, he heartily disliked Cary and his methods, although he later saw the value of Cary's training and sought to create a similar school in turn-of-the-century Newport News.

Although the memoirist minimized his formal education, his manuscript shows him to have had a good mind, sharpened by schooling and by observation. He was a man of common sense, practicality, ingenuity, modesty, and compassion. Though he was too indulgent of slavery and blind to shortcomings of Southern life, he accepted the verdict of Appomattox without bitterness. And though he disliked Collis Potter Huntington and his strong-arm business methods, he welcomed the Chesapeake and Ohio to Newport News in 1880 and became a potent figure in the city's rise. At the time of his death in 1917 he was one of the city's leading citizens.

Reading West's account of his harassed life after Federal forces landed at Newport News Point in 1861, one is bound to sympathize with the pudgy 22-year-old who became his family's mainstay. In spite of his parents' ill health and his sisters' dependency, George Ben West got the family safely to Richmond, helped them survive refugee hardships, and kept their hopes alive after they returned to their desolated Peninsula in 1865. No wonder he confessed to chronic nervous diarrhea in youth, or that he never married.

They cannot rank with such Confederate classics as Mary Boykin Chesnut's *A Diary from Dixie* or the Civil War letters from Georgia published as *The Children of Pride*, but George Ben West's memoirs offer an insight into the United States' most tragic war and the years that followed. In addition, they show the social revolution which followed the triumph of Yankee industry over Southern agriculture in 1865. The booming Newport News of today—a military-industrial complex of 150,000 people—has little in common with the acadian landscape which Federal troops infiltrated on May 27, 1861.

The new age had clearly arrived by April 1889, when Collis Huntington came to Newport News on his private rail car for the opening of the first drydock of his new Chesapeake Dry Dock and Construction Company. (It was another invasion, but this time a peaceable one.) With Huntington was the California poet, Joaquin Miller, who looked in vain for reminders of the *Monitor* and *Merrimac* or the other Civil War battles that had changed the world. Miller wrote:

> *And where are the monsters that tore this main?*
> *And where are the monsters that shook this shore?*
> *The sea grew mad: And the shore shot flame!*
> *The mad sea monsters they are no more.*
> *The palm, and the pine, and the sea sands brown;*
> *The far sea songs of the pleasure crews;*
> *The air like balm in this building town—*
> *And that is the picture of Newport News.*

George Ben West was in a unique spot to see the world of sailboats and horse-drawn wagons give way to the world of coal and steam and steel. There was no better place to see that change than in the Newport News of his lifetime. This is his account of what he saw.

CHAPTER I

A Few Incidents of Youth

I HAVE BEEN REQUESTED TO PUT DOWN IN WRITING some of my experiences, particularly during the War between the States and during Reconstruction days. And it has occurred to me that it might be well for myself to take a retrospection of all my past life, so as to be more fully impressed how good God has been to me, how He has led me; though I have rendered unto Him so little, and have been so rebellious, ungrateful, and unthankful, and have so little appreciated and taken advantage of the opportunities He has given me. May the writing of my recollections be the means of my doing more for the honor and glory of His great and holy name, and my taking advantage of the opportunities He is giving me; and make me more thankful and grateful for what He has done for me. I have heard old people say that in looking back to their childhood that it seemed but a short time; this is not so in my case, I seem to have lived hundreds of years, and so shall be able to recall probably only a very few of the incidents of youth.

I was born on the Newport News farm, then in Elizabeth City County, on January 10, 1839. The farm had been purchased by father about six or eight years before and he built the house in which I first saw the light; this house was on the river bank about Eleventh Street and Washington Avenue extended, near the centre of the riverfront of the farm. When I was about two years old, a Mrs. Sarah B. Watson, who had moved away from Warwick County some years before to Missouri with her husband and only living child, a son, returned alone, having lost both. For reasons I know not, she came to live at father's house.

She had been married three times and had lost a good many

children, most of them quite young. Her last husband had not been a kind one to her, and she lavished all her affections upon her boy, and he had now been buried in St. Louis, then in a far-off land. She was lonely and sad, with no one to look up to or look after her. She had some money and an old faithful slave, Aunt Peggy, who had been with her in all of her wanderings and in all her sorrows, who had preferred to remain a slave to becoming a free woman while in a free state. Mrs. Watson loaned my father $1,000, and he promised to take care of her for the interest on it. She loaned $500 to another party on a farm, the interest of which kept her in spending money. When my youngest sister was born, she was named Missouri by her. I was then taken by Mammy Watson to her room and from that day was nursed and petted and spoiled as an only child could be. I slept with her till quite a big boy and loved her as I did my own mother. All the love and affection of her ardent nature was lavished on me, from this time till her death in 1868. Mrs. Watson is buried just this side of North Newport News and between the railroad and the main road—Virginia Avenue extended. The grave is marked with a stone and enclosed with pipe in stone posts and enclosing her family.

I was about four years old when one Sunday I was put in the cart in which the older children were going to Hampton to the Sunday school, so that I might have a ride to the outer gate. I had my legs hanging out of the back of the cart. There being too much weight behind and the cart not tied down to the shafts, it was upset and one of my legs caught under the cart, and all the children were piled on me. The hip bone was dislocated, but I have no idea which hip it is. A messenger was sent to Hampton for a doctor. I remember the popping of the bone when it was pulled in place. I suppose I soon got well; I have no other recollection about it.

In the spring of '44 my sister Sarah died in Hampton of the measles and whooping cough. That session father had boarded the older children in Hampton to go to school; previous to this they had gone to a neighborhood school. I remember how sad I felt, and how solemn it was waiting in the yard of now the old Isaac Jones place (two miles out of Hampton) for the procession to come from Hampton. We (Missouri and I) were not carried to Hampton for fear we would catch the disease. She was buried at the West place near New Market.

I do not know whether father had thought of moving to Hampton before; even if he had, this hastened him. Though of very limited education, he at this time seemed determined to give his children the very best schooling he could afford or could be had. And he made for us the greatest sacrifices in order that we might be well educated. He had begun his married life with little means, and had begun to accumulate, and was well fixed on the farm and making money; yet he broke up his home, and remained himself on the farm and thus kept up two establishments. He always sent us to the best schools, no matter what the cost was. We first lived in rented houses, but in 1845 he bought a large lot, at the southeast corner of Hope and Queen (Main), in Hampton, on which he built a very large house, which he called a double house. The passages were through the centre without partitions; so both families (for he rented out half of it) had to use the same passages and staircases and, of course, had to be quite intimate; but we were fortunate in having nice families, and for us children it was very delightful. The lower story was used as stores.

In the spring of 1845 or '46 there was probably the highest tide in this section, with the exception perhaps of the April tide about 1891. The tide came up from the wharf in Hampton to Hope Street.

In January 1845 I was sent to school to Colonel John B. Cary, who then taught in what was called the old Courthouse. I did not know a letter, and although Colonel Cary was the best teacher I ever saw and could come down to the capacity of the dullest scholar, yet I doubt whether at this time he was a fit teacher for a beginner, on account of the fact he was a very strict disciplinarian, and as he had been teaching but a few years it was necessary, in order to convince the school that he was to be obeyed, for him to use the rod not sparingly. We younger ones were often so frightened by seeing the whipping of some one in a class which had just recited that we would miss our lessons, though we were prepared, and so be chastised. Mammy Watson always heard me recite my lessons before I went to school. Colonel Cary was kind to the smaller children in letting us go out of school often and in giving us fruit, which was often brought him by the country scholars. Yet we feared and hated him more than we loved him, but I doubt whether a teacher was ever more beloved than he by his scholars when they were grown.

I will give an instance of how severe he was. There were two rooms. The largest boys—young men really—were put in the smaller room and the little boys were also in this room, to be looked after by the older ones. On Christmas eve near time for school to close, Colonel Cary was hearing a lesson and out of sight of our room. One of the large boys threw a piece of coal at another, and soon several were engaged in the fun until the noise attracted the Colonel, who came in and thrashed every boy in the room, little and big. He whipped in the palm of the outstretched hand with a seasoned bamboo about the size of a pencil. This did not injure but was very severe, and the hands felt as if on fire, and we cooled them by putting them on our slates when we went to our seats.

The next session Colonel Cary taught in the old academy on Pee Dee, where is now [1899] the Hampton Academy. This property had been purchased by money gotten from property left about 1636 by Syms and Eaton for the education of the poor of the county. I expect this was the starting of the first free school in the United States. These old deeds, I think, are among the papers in the Hampton Courthouse. Father refused to send us to Cary because he thought the school should be kept as a free school only and no paid scholars should attend. He therefore sent me to Mr. William Hawkins, a Baptist preacher who, though not so strict, was much more passionate and consequently more unjust and unkind than Cary.

I think he taught only one session, and then I went to another preacher, a northern man named Wheeler who at first taught in the basement of the Baptist church. He incited us by rewards more than by punishment; every week he gave out two prizes—one to the smaller boys who behaved best and recited best, a piece of silver of what was called four pence—its value being 6¼ cents; to the larger scholars, a 25 cent piece. For reasons I do not know, he moved his school to Old Point and taught in one of the casemates of the fort [Monroe]. I and brother walked to the school from Hampton when we did not get a free ride in the steamboat or a hack, and we enjoyed the trip very much.

In the Presidential campaign of '48, I remember with what delight I engaged in the parades of the boys and the hoisting of the Whig pole (a persimmon), and the eating at the great barbeque at the Courthouse. This is the only barbeque I ever saw in Hampton, and I think the last ever had there. The boys as well as the men had their clubs and at night would turn out with transparencies, and some times we would get into fights, for we took as much interest in the elections as the voters.

In the spring of '48 or '49 there was a case of smallpox on the back street running to the Courthouse and so quite near us. I do not think I ever saw a person more afraid of this disease than father, except perhaps our family physician, Dr. Richard Banks. As soon as father learned of the case, he sent in all the conveyances and moved us all out on the farm at Newport News. How delighted we were, for we always spent all the time we could, both on Saturdays and holidays, in the country.

The farm house being rented to Mr. Dewbre (father of Mrs. W. J. Hawkins), who had also another daughter and two sons; we moved into a house near the creek. This house was one story and was built of sawed logs, weatherboarded on the outside, and insides the cracks plastered. It had only one large room downstairs and a wide hall, and two rooms in the roof, so we were greatly crowded and had to make partitions of quilts, but we greatly enjoyed the novelty. Frequently some of us would spend the night with the Dewbres or Parrishes. We remained four or five weeks and had a grand time. All the young people of the neighborhood would get together every day at the different houses and often on nice days picnic in the woods where we had put up a nice bush house. This case of smallpox was the only one.

In June '49 the cholera broke out in Hampton and surrounding county, and a great many persons died. Not a one of our family, either white or black, in Hampton or on the farm in Newport News, had an attack of it. Mr. John Hawkins' negroes had it very bad, and he lost several young negro men. I do not think there was any other case in the Newport News neighborhood. It was claimed that the disease was caused in the Hawkins' case by leaving some decayed potatoes in the cellar under the house, and some of the negroes slept in an adjoining room. Mr. Hawkins and family were greatly frightened and moved to Hampton in our house. Dr. Banks told father to let us eat the same food as usual but be sure to have all vegetables perfectly fresh and well cooked. Many persons almost starved themselves.

About this time father engaged in the shoe business in one of his stores and continued about ten years. He rented out half of his farm, and about 1854 brother took charge of the other half and carried on farming till father bought the Burk farm for him, at the mouth of Salter's Creek. In 1849 my sister Mary Emily married Mr. John Lee, who lived only three weeks after.

From 1850 to '55 I was sent to the free schools (in Hampton), and as the teachers were changed nearly every year and most of them were very poor teachers, my time was almost entirely thrown away. During this time as I did not study much I began to read such papers as the *New York Ledger* and all trashy novels I could get hold of and by this means lost the taste for more solid reading and for study. I was so fond of reading that I did not take the exercise I ought, and in the spring of '55 my liver became so torpid that I was quite sick, and when I was better the doctor advised father to send me to the farm at Newport News and let me walk or ride to the free school kept by Mr. William Crawford (near the Skinner place), where is now (1899) the oil tank.

Mr. Parkerson, who lived at the farmhouse on the river, had two children—a boy and a girl—who I usually waited for and accompanied to school. I stayed with my brother in the house before mentioned, near Salter's Creek. I enjoyed the change very much, and the exercise kept me well and strong. That summer the yellow fever broke out in Norfolk, and there was probably the worst epidemic ever in this country. Crawford, the teacher of the school, was a drinking man, and in one of his sprees that summer went over to Norfolk and presented himself as a physician and was shown some of the worst cases in the city. Being accustomed to stop with us in Hampton, when he returned from Norfolk late in the evening, he went directly to the room he usually occupied, without seeing any of the family or servants.

The next morning he was found sick, and his sickness was the yellow fever. I was out on the farm at Newport News and did not know it till the evening he died, when I came back to Hampton. I think he lived only two days from the time he came to the house; fortunately probably his room was in the attic. Coffins were not then kept on hand, so as soon as the doctor said he would live but a few hours, his coffin was ordered and preparations made for his burial. He died about bedtime and was at once buried in the St. John's churchyard, in sight of the window where we stood.

It is the only burial I ever saw at night and was exceedingly sad and impressive, and I remember with what awe I watched the lights in the graveyard as the sad and silent procession moved to the grave. It was no doubt one of the smallest processions that ever accompanied a corpse to the grave but to me the most impressive burial I ever witnessed. Crawford was one of the most gifted and talented men ever raised in

Hampton presented this appearance to the French naturalist August Plee, who visited Virginia in 1821. A windmill stands amid mansions around Hampton Creek.

or around Hampton and was also very highly educated, but his life was a failure on account of his appetite for liquor. He was also a man of high social standing and had many relatives in Hampton. There were probably a dozen other cases of fever in and around Hampton among the refugees from Norfolk, but in no instance was a case contracted from them.

Colonel Cary had built a private academy [on Pee Dee Point, facing Hampton Creek], on the lot now occupied by the Baptist parsonage and other houses, so father again sent me to him that fall of '55, and I remained with him till the fall of '59 when I entered the University of Virginia. I was not as far advanced as boys of my age, and for two sessions I had to study very hard, for I always liked to stand well in my classes. On January 18, 1857 commenced the greatest snowstorm in my recollection and perhaps the coldest spell. It commenced on Saturday to snow; Sunday was very cold and snowing with a heavy gale blowing. Father had his winter supply of wood in the yard with about a ten foot fence around it. The wind was so strong that the fence began to give way, and he had me out in the storm for a short time, propping up the fence. I do not remember that I was ever so cold. Monday morning the snow on the north side of the streets was up to the second story windows, and persons had to tunnel through it to get out of their houses; on the south side there was scarcely any. It was still very cold. Billie Stores and I went to school on Tuesday, had very little trouble in getting there, but when we reached the schoolhouse yard we were met by the boarders (scholars), who had dug a cave in the snow and they threatened to put us in it if we did not at once return home. They wished a holiday and knew if the town boys came, Mr. Cary would open school. We remained only a few minutes and did not go again for several days. In those days there were no wood and coal yards in Hampton. Those who were able bought their winter supply in the fall. The rest depended on their supply of wood from the country people, who daily hauled it in. Persons became almost panic-stricken for fear there would be a wood famine, and offered as much as $20 a cord for wood. Father had many offers but told all that when their wood gave out he would share with them but would not sell any.

Dr. Sam Sheilds, who owned the Little England farm, fortunately had hundreds of cords racked up where John Willis now lives, and before night was delivering it in town. It should be recorded to his praise that he did not charge more for it than he could have gotten for it in ordinary weather. His supply lasted till the country people could come in, which was some time, for the snow drifted between the fences along the country roads, and the roads were not used for two months, but in a week or ten days by going out in the fields, the people could get to town.

It was also several weeks before there was any intercourse with Norfolk or Baltimore, but I heard of no fear of lack of food, so I suppose the town was well supplied with groceries. It was said that a party walked from Norfolk to Hampton on the ice, crossing from the Rip Raps to Old Point by jumping on blocks of ice. The current is so strong there that it is probable the channel was not entirely closed, but it was feasible for a person to cross who had the daring to undertake it. I could not get to the Newport News farm to see the ice in the James River, but from our attic could see it in Hampton Roads, and the piles of ice there presented truly an arctic scene. One day with a party I ascended the steeple of St. John's Church and viewed Hampton Roads with a spy glass, and I have never forgotten what to me seemed mountains of ice.

Cary made his a military school when he moved into his new academy; he had also a female department attached and employed a female teacher. Some of the larger girls were in the boys' classes and came into our room to recite, so also some of the smaller boys went in the girls' room to recite in the classes with the young girls. I think this arrangement a most excellent one, for it created a sort of rivalry between the boys and the girls. Cary was always anxious for us to have the advantages of any entertainment or lecture that would be instructive to us and would often employ lecturers himself and have them given to the school free.

John Cary's Hampton Academy, built facing Hampton Creek, educated George Benjamin West in the old-fashioned "3 Rs."

GEORGE BENJAMIN WEST began writing his memoirs in 1899 in response to friends and family. He wrote in ink in a small, neat script which is legible in all but a few cases. The narrative is chronological, but the author occasionally returned to add details or to correct some name or date he had found to be in error. The present division of the text into paragraphs and chapters was made by the editor. In a few cases, lapses of spelling, grammar, and punctuation have been corrected and a few identifying details added to the text.

At about the time George Ben West began the memoirs, he moved to a three-storied Victorian house at Thirty-fourth Street and West Avenue which he had built to house him, his sister Missouri West Smith, and her daughter and son-in-law, Mr. and Mrs. William E. Barrett. George Ben West died in 1917, and the West residence was demolished in the 1940s. West Avenue, named for the West family and once Newport News' prime residential area, is now largely parking space for downtown Newport News shoppers and employees of the shipyard.

The farm of Parker West, which fronted in 1861 on the James River from the easternmost extremity at Point Breeze northwestward to the present Eighteenth Street, was then in the "toe" of Elizabeth City County, which encompassed much of present downtown industrial Newport News, southwest of Salter's Creek. This "toe" was transferred by the Virginia General Assembly in 1882 from Elizabeth City County to Warwick County, and in 1896 part of it became the incorporated city of Newport News, created out of Warwick County.

Parker West had a second farm at New Market in Elizabeth City County, near the intersection of West Queen Street and Briarfield Road in Hampton, referred to in this chapter as the burial place of Sarah West, the author's sister, who died in 1844 of the measles and whooping cough. He owned a third farm called Casey's and about two dozen scattered houses in Hampton and Elizabeth City. Most of these properties were lost to him during the Civil War and Reconstruction, as his son recounts.

These memoirs contain constant references to the author's family, who were numerous and close. His father, Parker West, had married an Eastern Shore neighbor, Mary Drummond Bell, and they had seven children. Of the five daughters, only two married: Mary Emily, the second eldest, who married William P. Marrow of Hampton and became the mother of four children; and Missouri, or Sue, who married Robert Mortimer Smith of King and Queen County and had two daughters. One of these, Emily, lived to maturity, marrying attorney William Edwards Barrett of Newport News in 1892. George Ben West's only brother was William Drummond West, who died unmarried during the Civil War, in 1862.

Throughout his memoirs West alludes to Mrs. Sarah Watson, a widow who lived at his parents' house and lavished maternal affection on him. He refers to her as "Mammy Watson," the "mammy" meaning nurse or nanny. On her death she left her estate to young West. She seems to have been closer to him than his mother, who was ill during much of Wests youth and died when he was 23. Born in 1794, she died in the West household in 1868, leaving West all her worldly goods.

West's most influential teacher was John Baytop Cary, referred to as Colonel Cary for his service to the Confederacy, rising to the rank of lieutenant colonel. Born in Elizabeth City County on October 18, 1819, Cary graduated from William and Mary with a degree in civil engineering and taught in a free school in Hampton. In 1852 he founded Hampton Military Academy, where West prepared for college. At the outbreak of the Civil War, Cary was given the rank of major in Virginia's forces and placed in charge of Hampton's defense. After the war, Cary remained in Richmond as an insurance agent. He served by appointment of Governor Fitzhugh Lee as Richmond's unpaid superintendent of schools. A Richmond public school today bears his name.

The "old Courthouse" in Hampton where Cary taught young West in 1845 was near St. John's Church, and "the old academy on Pee Dee" where he taught in 1846 was near Hampton Creek and north of Queen Street, near the Hampton municipal building opened in 1977. The "property left about 1636 by Syms and Eaton" to which West refers was the 1634 bequest of Benjamin Syms and the 1659 bequest of Thomas Eaton, both for free schools in Elizabeth City County, the first in British America. The legacies were recalled in Hampton's recent Syms-Eaton elementary school.

The Presidential campaign of 1848 which West mentions pitted

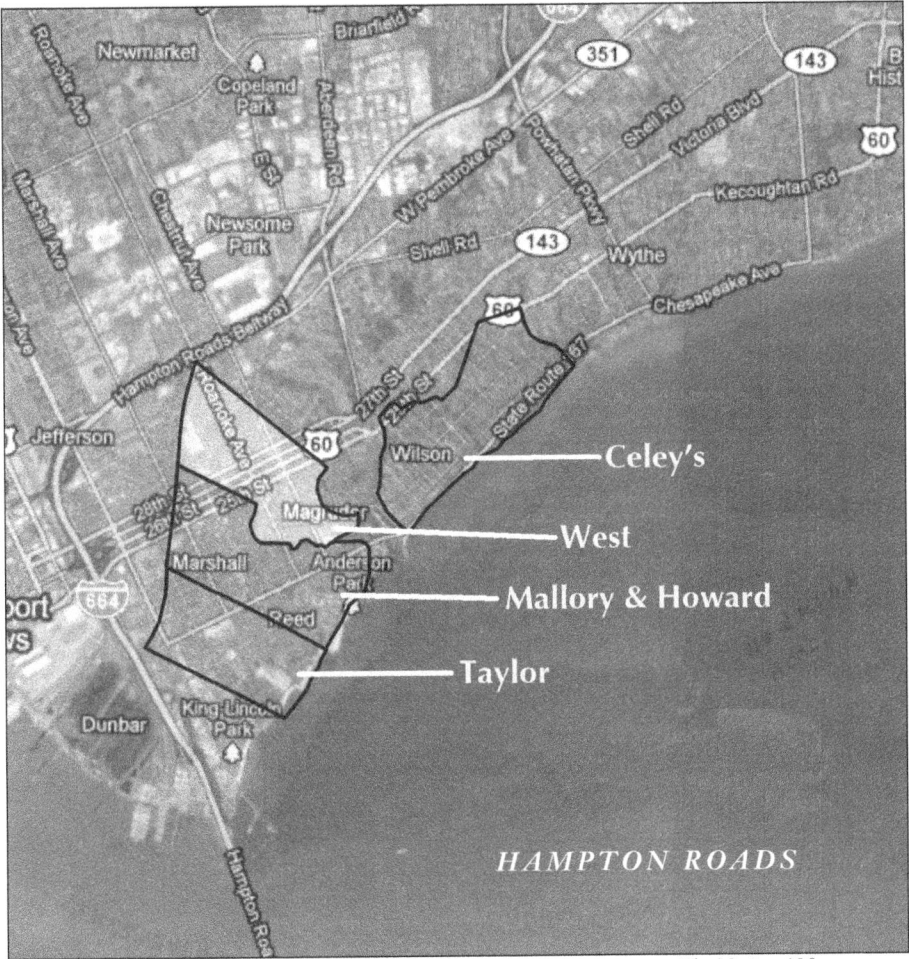

*A present-day map, overlaid on a map from 1870, shows the relative area
of landholdings during West's time. The former Parker West farm occupied
parts of Newport News Point, then part of Elizabeth City County.*

the Whigs' Zachary Taylor against the Democrats' Lewis Cass. The
"transparencies" displayed in nocturnal demonstrations were transparent signs which were backlighted and hoisted on poles by parading
Democrats and Whigs.

Dr. Richard Banks, the West family's physician in Hampton, was
owner of a Hampton Hotel and gave his name to Banks Street.

The free schools West attended 1850-55 were those endowed by the gifts of Syms, Eaton, and others. Hampton was one of the few localities in Virginia which had created a public or "free" school system under an Act of Assembly of 1845. The Syms-Eaton Academy joined it in 1852.

The John Willis living in Hampton in 1899 was John Middleton Willis, for 45 years superintendent of Hampton public schools, publisher of the weekly Hampton *Monitor*, and an attorney.

Little England Farm, the residence of Dr. Sam Sheilds, was on the west shore of Hampton River. The Hampton Yacht Club now occupies part of the farm's property.

The frigid winter of 1857, which froze the surface of Hampton Roads, was not uncommon in West's lifetime; a similar freeze occurred in 1917–18.

The Rip Raps was the Hampton Roads shoal which was built up and fortified by the Army in the 1830s as Castle Calhoun, an outpost of Fort Monroe. It is now inactive. During the Civil War its name was changed to Fort Wool. In 1967 the fort was abandoned by the United States government and ownership reverted to Virginia, which leased it to the City of Hampton for possible development. In 2011 Fort Monroe was demobilized as an Army base, and will be developed for private and public uses, including by the National Park Service.

Hampton History Museum

Buildings and cranes on the "Rip-Raps," circa 1860.

CHAPTER II

A Good Deal of Amusement

IN THE SPRING — ON MAY 13, 1857 — THERE WAS a celebration at Jamestown Island in memory of the landing of the English in America. It was quite a large affair and was participated in by the military of the State. Cary chartered the steamboat *Star* to take us scholars up, and as he wished to show us Williamsburg also, we went up the river the day before the celebration, landed at the Kingsmill wharf, and were met with a few wagons which carried the smaller boys. We larger ones had to foot it, and I thought it the longest three miles I ever saw. The citizens had prepared for us a dinner in Colonel Robert Armistead's yard; it was a good dinner and I am sure we all did full justice to the hospitality of the old city.

Our military instructor was James Massenburg who, though he had no military training, took great pride in drilling us boys and thought we were the best drilled company in the State. In the afternoon we paraded the town and were invited by the Superintendent of the Lunatic Asylum to drill in the yard, he thinking it would please the inmates to see us. Most of them may have been pleased, but some of them were rendered wild and furious and became so violent as necessitated their confinement. We were carried through some of the wards, and I remember seeing a poor fellow coming from the shower bath and he was the most miserable person I think I ever saw. We were quartered in the college and in private houses in the town. I spent the night with a few others with the aunt of Mrs. Stores, a Mrs. Mason, who lived nearly opposite the old Bruton Parish Episcopal Church. The ravings of the insane kept me awake nearly all night. The next morning we returned to the wharf in wagons and took the *Star* to the island.

As there was no wharf, we had to land in small boats. Never perhaps

Boat traffic on the James River during the Jamestown 250th celebration, from **Harper's Weekly, June 27, 1857.**

were there so many boats anchored off the island and all decorated with flags, and they and the soldiers and crowds of people presented a very gay and lively scene. There was no place to drill, as the field was in wheat nearly knee high; so all the military formed and took position around the grandstand, where we stood at least four hours, listening to the addresses.

Ex-President John Tyler delivered the address, and our own Hampton poet James Barron Hope recited a poem. It was truly a stirring and inspiring sight to see so many people embarking in small boats to their respective steamers and schooners and on that beautiful May evening. It had been nearly 250 years since there had been so much life around the island, if ever. It is to be hoped that in 1907 there will be witnessed a much larger and grander demonstration.

Massenburg had had no opportunity to show us off to the large crowd and was much disappointed. So when we all got aboard he marshalled us on the upper deck, which was very small and narrow, and put us through the manual, hoping no doubt that we should be noticed by the passengers of some of the many boats. He stood in our front and was only a foot or two from the muzzle of our muskets when we took aim. Our guns were loaded with blank cartridges, as all the military were saluting. In giving the command "Ready, Aim, Fire," he either said "Fire" in his excitement, or we misunderstood the command, and the whole company pulled trigger. He was very much frightened and liked to have jumped overboard. Fortunately, those in his immediate front had the presence of mind to turn their muskets enough to keep from firing on him and burning him. We enjoyed his fright very much. We prided ourselves on exact obedience to orders and insisted he gave the command to fire. After he recovered his fright and saw he was not hurt, he was pleased and gratified that we should obey a command when given, though we knew a mistake was made in giving the order.

We arrived in Hampton about 11 o'clock that night, and it seemed to me the whole town and country turned out to receive us. We had been gone nearly two days, and parents and friends were a little anxious and came down to welcome us and to see if all were safe. I do not remember a single accident or mishap except the one mentioned above, and that had afforded us a good deal of amusement. It was one of the most enjoyable trips of my life.

In the summer of '56 or '57 the steam frigate *Colorado* came into Hampton Roads and was visited by many persons. Colonel Cary took our school out to see her. The boys went in uniform and carried their guns, and of course, Mr. Massenburg wished to show us off to the officers and crew. It happened that the captain was in Norfolk, and when he returned and found us drilling on the quarterdeck, he was very angry with the officer in command for allowing us under arms on the deck, and we were soon dismissed. He said it was an unheard of occurrence.

The same year we went over to Norfolk to the fair and marched out to the grounds which were north of the city. We participated in a flag presentation and remained in line the whole day because Mr. Massenburg got off with some officers and got tight. We did not see anything of the exhibits, nor did we get anything to eat. I never before or since have been so tired and worn out. I do not think Colonel Cary could have gone over with us or he would have seen to our comfort and entertainment. Massenburg regretted his neglect very much and apologized to us. We boys all were fond of him and knew his neglect was on account of his fondness for liquor.

Colonel Cary had a debating society for his boys, and he made the boarders join and most of the day scholars, but somehow or other I was not compelled till the last year. I was naturally diffident, and not being as far advanced as some boys of my age added to it. So I dreaded to become a member of the society, but at last Cary so insisted upon it that I had to join. I really enjoyed the meetings till he insisted on my declaiming a piece. There was no way to get out of it, so I prepared a piece and thought I had it perfectly.

When I was called on and got on the platform, I could not remember a word of the piece. It seemed to me I stood there five minutes before I remembered a word and began to recite. I could not have looked very much frightened, though I was terribly so. The piece I cannot now remember, but it was such a selection that the pause before beginning was very appropriate, and Cary and the boys all thought that I so intended, and I was highly congratulated by the colonel, but I knew I did not deserve the praise. I do not think I ever attempted to declaim again. I am now very sorry that Cary had not made me join the society when I first entered the school and [had not] made me declaim often, for it might have given me some courage and confidence, but the feeling has grown upon me. I cannot express myself now intelligibly, on my feet, before the fewest number of people in any kind of meeting.

Colonel Cary had gotten the reputation of being very strict, and all knew he had to be obeyed, so there was very little of disobedience to his rules or missing of lessons. He adopted the plan of keeping in after school those who deserved punishment, and so the school did not see the correction. He had perfect order in his school, and had painted on the wall in front of the desks: "Order is Heaven's first Law." We were also required to keep an oil rag in the desks to keep them rubbed up bright every day, and remove all scratches made by our brass buttons, so that his desks looked new after they had been used several years. He was a great blessing to all this section and has left his impress upon the hearts and characters of most of his scholars. I have always thought that had he returned to Hampton and opened his school after the war, it would have been one of the greatest blessings this section could have received. He told me that he loved teaching better than anything else, but he could not afford to open a school in Hampton, so he remained in Richmond and engaged in the insurance business, and I am glad to say made money out of it.

Father was very indulgent with us and never minded expense when we could see anything instructive or even amusing, so we went to all places that were fit for us to go. He loved his children dearly, but he did not show it by fondling us as much as by gratifying our wishes whenever he thought them proper. If he said "No" it was of no use

An idyllic waterfront appears in this illustration of "Newport News, Va., now in possession . . . of Federal Troops" appears in **Leslie's Illustrated Newspaper,** *June 15, 1861.*

to try to induce him to change his mind by fretting or crying. I don't think he ever whipped me except two or three times and then for refusing to take medicine when I was quite young. I had a great aversion to taking medicine and have not entirely gotten over it.

I will mention an incident when I was about six years old. The doctor had been called in, though I could not have been very sick. I refused to swallow the dose. I could not be induced by all sorts of promises or presents offered, so after this failure it became necessary to use force, and all the servants called in to give it. I was stretched out on the trundle bed, one holding my head, one at each arm, and the cook holding my two feet. The medicine was in a tablespoon to be poured down. I shut my mouth tight, someone held my nose, and it seemed there was no chance and that I must take it. But I began to draw up my feet, and the cook let me do it, and just as I had to open my mouth, my legs were sufficiently bent to have a good purchase and I let them fly at the cook and knocked her over, and this deferred taking the dose. They at once sent again for the doctor, and when he arrived I knew from previous experiences that I would have to take it. But though he was a large man and I somewhat feared him, I would not take it till he held my nose so long that I had to open my mouth and take it.

Children do not seem to have worms now as they did in my youth. Every year we had to take worm medicine, and not in the form of candy, but wormseed tea, and you had to drink a teacup of it. I remember well when wormifuge was introduced. It tasted no better but only required a teaspoonful. I well remember the last dose I took, and even now when thinking of it I imagine I can still taste it. I sat at the foot of the dining room table, all the family standing around trying to persuade me to take it and offering me all sorts of presents, and these were put on the table to tempt me. The table was full of all kind of good things, and at last some special present made me succumb, and I swallowed the nauseous stuff.

When we first moved to Hampton I and brother had quite a narrow escape of having a broken limb, if not a broken head. Father had sent in from the country a carload of vegetables, and after they were taken out, brother and I got into the cart. We spied a potato in the dirt in the cart near the tail board and both went for it. The cart, not being tied down, turned completely over and caught us under it, and as the board was in, we were in utter darkness under the cart body. It seems even now that for us to have been so caught without having either an arm or leg caught by the sides or ends of the cart was wonderful. We were much frightened but escaped with only our eyes full of dirt.

I took my first chew of tobacco at school in the old Courthouse. One of the large boys gave it to me in school. It did not take long to make me sick. Fortunately, my paleness was noticed by Cary, and when I told him I was sick, he told me to go out in the yard. I threw away the quid, and soon the air restored me. When I returned and told Cary what had made me sick, he gave that boy such a thrashing he did not soon forget, and I do not think he ever tried the joke on another boy.

The next chew I remember was several years after. Mammy Watson smoked the pipe, which then was done much more frequently than now by ladies, and she smoked the plug tobacco, I suppose because it was stronger, or they may not have manufactured the smoking tobacco as now. I was sent over to buy a plug for her, and I noticed that a piece of the other plug adhered to the plug given me, so I pulled it off, and after delivering the plug went behind the kitchen and sat on an old work bench that had been left by the carpenters when building the house, and began to chew. I was soon stretched out very sick and, being found and carried up to bed, someone was about to be dispatched for the doctor. They had no doubt I was very ill and no idea what the matter was. With the dread of having to take some vile medicine, I confessed to what had made me sick. I believe that was the last chew of tobacco I ever took.

I have always been surprised that I never smoked, as I had the example of Mammy Watson and was raised in her room, which had always the odor of smoke. I also was taught very early to smoke. Mr. Sam Lively, who boarded with us while he worked on the house father built, was very fond of me, and on Sundays when he went out to New Market his home would take me along and always gave me a mild cheroot to smoke. They never made me sick. (I was then a little over six years old.) Father did not use tobacco in any form, nor ever had liquor in his house, and I suppose his opposition kept me from these things.

When I was about eight years old father had some business on the Eastern Shore, and he took me over with him. We went in a pungy, and the wind must have been contrary, for we anchored that night in a creek between Gloucester and Mathews Counties, in Mobjack Bay. It was in March, and there were a great many oyster boats anchored in the creek, and the lights on the boats and the passing of the small boats and the songs and hollering of the oystermen impressed me very much, and I was delighted. On this trip I had my first seasickness. The next day I was on deck and felt sick but did not know what the matter was, so I went into the cabin, but I grew worse and returned again to the deck. I only remained a few moments and then down to the cabin again. This was kept up till I was noticed by the cook, who was in the cabin and put me in a berth, and I was soon relieved by rendering my tribute to the sea.

One day after our arrival in crossing a hard marsh, father and someone were talking and I was walking behind. They came to a ditch and jumped across with no thought of me. When I came up I thought it too wide to jump, and then I thought if father, who was quite low and very stout, could, that I ought to, and so I attempted it and went in up to my shoulders. I was taken to a house nearby that seemed to me to be filled with boys, and I was soon fitted out in one of their suits. I think any size boy could have been fitted at this house. The day we were to return home was very cold, and we had to ride a long distance to take the boat, so I was told to warm my feet well. Instead of taking

Small dwellings surrounded Hampton Creek when George Ben West attended school there in the 1850s. This view was made near Queen Street.

off my shoes, I put them to the fire, so when I went to the carriage I could hardly walk, my shoes burned me so, and on the ride I had only to bear on the sole and my feet got warm. I did not suffer from cold feet, but both soles came off my shoes.

I have all my life had a great aversion of going to see the sick. Instead of this being corrected in my youth, one incident caused the family not to try again. One of my playmates was sick, and mother and mammy insisted that I should go to see him, and after they had determined on it there was no use to try to get off. So I was sent. When I returned they asked me if John was sick much and I said "Yes!" "What is the matter with him?" "Scarlet fever." They were very much alarmed when I told them I was allowed to go in, to sit by his bed and remain some time in the room. I did not take the fever, but I was never again forced to go to see the sick; I very much rejoiced that John had the scarlet fever.

Like all boys, I was very fond of going barefooted and often disobeyed by taking off my shoes at school so as to run better; but I was early punished for it. In running around an office where cinders had been thrown, I trod upon a clinker that cut my foot fearfully and laid me up many weeks. I was also severely punished for my disobedience in violating the sabbath, and came very near losing my life.

I and three other boys, the oldest only about 13 years old, went out sailing in a canoe on Sunday. The older boy was the only one that knew anything about a sailboat. We started for Old Point but after getting out of the creek fortunately turned back, as it was blowing very hard. When we got within 100 yards of the Hampton Wharf, Joe, the captain said "Let's go up to the bridge," and we agreed. I held the sheetrope line and was sitting on the wash board. He said "Watch out, I am going to jibe." I had not the remotest idea what he meant, but I said "jibe ahead." The next thing I knew was the sensation of sinking, and when I struck the bottom I realized I was overboard and made a struggle and shot up to the surface.

The boat was 100 or more feet from me, the sail flapping, and Joe with the paddle he had been steering with, trying to paddle to me. The younger boy was crying and the other trying to rip up a seat so as to use as a paddle. I at once realized it would take some time for them to reach me. I could not swim but began to try to keep up by trying it dog fashion, as we boys said, but my exertions were too violent, and I became so tired that I had to cease kicking. Then I would begin to sink, and when I heard the water go over my head I would struggle again and rise to the surface. This occurred a great many times. There were many people on the Hampton Wharf and at Burcher's Hotel but no boat near for them to rescue. They all thought I would be drowned, but I was not frightened so much as to stop my struggles.

At last a gentleman eating in a house where Daniel Marrow's now stands was informed by a boy in the yard that some one was overboard, but this was not so unusual as to make any impression, till he came up the second time and reported he was drowning. Then he rushed down to the landing, pushed down a punt, and came to me. My back was to him, and I knew nothing of his efforts till he had me by the hair. The canoe came up in a few minutes, and I was pulled in. I was so weak that I had to lie in the bottom of the boat, but when we landed I walked home. I was very much humiliated going up the street in such a condition on Sunday. No one at home knew of the accident till I walked in. It seemed to me I spit up a keg of water that evening; I don't think I could have held more than I had in me.

When about twelve years old father took me and mother to Baltimore to visit cousin Levin Drummond; he continued on to Lynn, Massachusetts to buy his shoe stock. I had heard a great deal about the Baltimore plugs and imagined I would certainly have to fight some of them. Unfortunately, a few days before we left I had knocked my right thumb out of joint in a boxing match, and it was so sore I had to carry my hand on my breast as it hurt to let it hang down, so I was in no condition for fighting. I was very much surprised to find the boys so gentlemanly and amiable. I had no doubt heard of the boys that frequented the slums, and I did not come in contact with them.

On this trip I went to the theatre for the first time, but before the end of the performance I was very much shocked by an actor offering up a prayer on the stage. I have never frequented the theatre often, and with one or two exceptions have had my religious feelings (though not a Christian) always hurt, and this is the reason I never liked it and disapproved of theatre going.

I was always fond of visiting the country, and spent every Saturday and all the holidays I could on the farm, or at Mr. Ned Parrish's, Hawkins', or Uncle Robert Davis' near New Market. I remember one Saturday a lot of the neighborhood boys went in bathing in New Market Creek. After dressing, I attempted to put on my shoes but could not get them on. I thought it because my feet were swollen, so I started to Hampton barefooted, stopping several times to put on the shoes, but they were so tight I could not keep them on. After passing the crossroads, I put them on. The next morning Billie Stores sent in for his shoes; I had taken his and left mine which were two sizes larger. I suffered excruciating pain while I had them on.

While I was going to Old Point to school, the Hope and Jones (James Barron Hope and John Pembroke Jones) duel took place. At recess, having heard it was to be at the sandhills, we went up the ramparts and saw the smoke from the pistols, but the men were hidden behind the sandhills. The posse of county officers and some officers from the fort we saw galloping up the beach, but the shots were fired before they arrived.

General Winfield Scott visited Fort Monroe, and with the tall plume in his cocked hat he towered high above the commanding General Bankhead, who was quite a large and tall man. Scott was the largest man I ever saw except a giant on exhibition named Angus McCaskin, who was seven and a half feet tall and well made.

I was always very fond of hunting and whenever in the country would roam the fields and the woods with a gun on my shoulder, but I never went possum hunting but once. I had walked from Hampton to Newport News with brother and R. A. Davis, our cousin and boon companion, when someone proposed a possum hunt, and we got the dogs and a few negro boys and started and roamed the woods till after midnight. After we got a long distance from the house, my legs began to hurt me, I suppose because I was tired, but I had what we called growing pains and so I dragged myself through the woods in almost excruciating pain. I then made a vow if I ever got home, they would never get me to join another possum hunt, so-called, for we did not even see a possum.

Not a great while after this I went coon hunting. It was Christmas time and we were again in the country, and all the neighborhood boys, about six or eight, came by the house hunting. I think there was with them as many dogs as boys. An old negro man, who had one of our slaves as a wife and who had previously gotten permission from father, proposed that we would remain around the premises while he cut down a very large hollow tree that grew across the creek. He said that none of the negroes went out possum hunting but that the dogs always treed something up this tree, but as it was full of hollows they could never get anything out, though he was sure it was full of coons and possums and as now there were so many of us and as many dogs, it would be impossible for anything to get away. When he had most cut through the tree, he called us. Brother, Bob, and I also each took a dog along, about ten boys and ten dogs, and we expected at least a dozen varmints. Though I was one of the smallest, I had the biggest dog. We were all stationed so as to be near the top when the tree fell but far enough off not to be hurt; each boy held his dog to keep him from running under the tree. My dog had no collar, so I got on his back and held him around the neck. When the tree began to crack, my dog became excited and I held on, but he was too strong and so soon threw me. When I got up there was such a barking and hollering that one would have thought the tree was full of coons, but as a fact there was only one and he quite small, so he had very little chance for his life, and really there was no coon fight—the odds were too great. We were very much disappointed but had had some fun. The old negro was completely crestfallen. Having spent half a day cutting down the tree, his reward was very small.

I remember an incident with a dog that was not so funny. I was on the farm at Newport News with mother, and starting out with a gun, she asked me to go across Newport News Creek on the Jack Parrish side and look for her flock of geese. She raised a great many white geese, for their feathers principally; and in the fall turned them out in the pasture around the marsh. Between the marsh and the cultivated fields there were usually thickets growing. I was followed by a little black and tan terrier, and in going through a thicket I came upon Mr. Parrish's hogs, quite a large number. Being kept away from the house, they were half wild, and when I walked up they began to grunt and chase the dog, who for protection ran up to me. I thought they would certainly bite me, but I cocked the gun, intending to shoot if they did bite, and with the muzzle fought them and backed till I got to the fence, where the little dog soon got through. I expect I was as scared as the dog. I do not know what effect the discharge of the gun would have had on the hogs, but I did not want to kill one and did not wish to waste a load by firing in the air.

One day brother came to town to spend the day; he was then living on the farm. Mother asked me to drive her out in his buggy as she wanted to take a trip. We had not gotten out of town before the bolt holding one of the shafts to the axle came out, and the shaft striking on the horse's heels, he began to run, pulling one shaft and going sideways. The buggy was soon upset, and we fell in its top. Mother had some earthen milk basins she was taking to the farm, and they were broken and one of them cut her throat. We were not dragged far, as the harness broke. I was a little stunned and had one side of the face skin rubbed off.

When I extricated myself and saw mother bleeding from the cut and in a faint, I thought she was dead. The gash was of very little depth, but quite long, and she soon recovered, but the whole town was stirred up by the accident. By her gentle nature, unselfish disposition, and unwearied kindnesses she was universally loved, both by white and black. I think there was hardly a family that did not come or send to enquire about her.

The young men of Hampton were accustomed to play some right expensive jokes sometimes. I remember once they took quite a large sloop and carried it up to King and Queen streets, and the owner had the expense of getting it back. Taking gates to other lots and moving signs was of frequent occurrence. One day a negro who was an habitual drunkard was found drowned. That night everyone who sold liquor had a piece of crepe tacked to his door and a notice inviting him to the funeral of this old man the next day as one of their "finished jobs." There was great indignation among the liquor dealers, and offers of rewards, and threats of what they would do if they found the guilty parties. I think the whole town enjoyed the joke and thought it deserved.

Papa Willis as we children called him (the Rev. J. M. Willis, grandfather of John M. Willis) would rather marry a couple than eat when hungry. He was called on at all times and by all sorts of people, for he was very much beloved by old and young, white and black. He kept a grocery in one of the stores in our house, and often when I would be in father's store he would call me in to witness a marriage, sometimes even before breakfast. I remember a marriage of negroes he took me to. It was between free negroes. The groom was a waterman and well known and beliked. The father of the bride was a slave but highly respected. A good many of the white men of the town attended the ceremony. The parson and I remained to the supper, to which we did full justice. We sat down first and were waited on, and left before the rest had theirs served; it was quite a swell affair.

I remember a trip to Mathews County to a camp meeting. I went with a Mr. Joynes who lived in our house. It was on Sunday. The excursion was from Norfolk, and we took the boat from Old Point. The camp ground was three miles from the wharf. No one was allowed to sell anything that day, and as our party had no invitation to dinner, we feared we would have to go dinnerless, but after awhile found an old slave from Hampton who had carried a lot of things to sell, and we soon had a good dinner prepared by him in his tent, for which we paid him well.

On our return to the wharf in a farm wagon, the seats broke down and there was no way to fix them, so rails were taken from the fence and put across the wagon to ride on. This was my only ride on a rail, and I enjoyed it. But when I got out at the boat and found I had worn out the seat of my pants and had on only a jacket that would not hide the seat, I got to a seat on the boat as soon as I could and had to so remain in it till it got dark.

IN May 1857 the Commonwealth of Virginia celebrated the 250th anniversary of Jamestown's settlement with a three-day observance, which West describes. It was the subject of an article in *Harper's Weekly* for June 27, 1857. The speaker was ex-President John Tyler, and the poet was James Barron Hope. Kingsmill wharf, where Cary's students debarked on May 12 for their tour of Williamsburg, was on the James River frontage of Kingsmill plantation near the entrance to College Creek.

Colonel Robert Armistead, whose yard was the site of the Hampton students' supper, was a Williamsburg attorney and a farmer of James City County. He lived in the vicinity of the present Matthew Whaley School in Williamsburg. His great-grandson, Robert Armistead, served as judge of the Williamsburg-James City Circuit Court from 1956 until 1977. The home still stands in Williamsburg.

James Massenburg, who taught at John B. Cary's school, descended from an early settler, Josiah Massenburg, a taxpayer in Warwick County in 1782.

The Lunatic Asylum, later to become Eastern State Hospital, vied in 1857 with the College of William and Mary for first importance in Williamsburg. Begun in 1773 as the first public mental institution in America, it fronted on Francis Street several hundred yards west of the present Williamsburg Inn. After the present Eastern State Hospital was built in the 1950s and '60s at Dunbar Farm, west of Williamsburg, the Francis Street buildings were torn down.

The pungy (from "Pungoteague") in which Parker West and his son sailed to the Eastern Shore was a small schooner-rigged vessel of a type developed on the Eastern Shore and long common in Virginia.

Daniel Marrow's house, near which George Benjamin West nearly drowned in Hampton Creek, stood on Bully's Point, now the site of Bridge Street and the Darling Bridge in Hampton.

The Baltimore plugs young West expected to fight were "plug-uglies," or city ruffians.

The duel between James Barron Hope and John Pembroke Jones took place on April 26, 1849, at Buckroe Beach. Both were wounded but recovered and became friends.

General Winfield Scott was supreme commander of the U.S. Army from 1841 till 1861. A native of Dinwiddie County, Virginia, he briefly attended the College of William and Mary in his youth.

General James Bankhead commanded Fort Monroe from 1848 until 1853.

The Rev. John M. Willis, referred to as "Papa Willis," was a Hampton minister of the early 19th century. His son, William Royall Willis, was a Confederate officer in the Civil War and later an attorney and Elizabeth City County judge. His grandson, John M. Willis, was superintendent of schools in the county, an attorney, and publisher of a Hampton weekly newspaper, *The Monitor.*

The camp meeting in Mathews County was a summer religious and social gathering of a type then popular with Baptists, Methodists, and other evangelistic sects.

USA Gen. James Bankhead and USA Gen. Winfield Scott

CHAPTER III

Not a Thought of the Future

IN 1856 OR '57 A TERRIFIC HAILSTORM AND hurricane passed over Hampton about 11 at night. Windows at that time had glass only about the size of 10 by 12 inches. The hail played havoc with the glass; over 200 were broken out in our house, and the noise of the wind and thunder and lightning and breaking glass was very awe-inspiring. We had a good many young ladies stopping with my sisters, and they became very much frightened, and some said the judgment day had come, but someone suggested that the judgment day could not come at night. This created such a laugh that they became more quiet.

In June '58 the Baptist General Assembly was held in Hampton and father entertained a great many delegates, as they did not ask (as now very often) only one to be put in a room or at least only one in a bed. Some of our rooms had six or eight. We also entertained a good many lady visitors. I enjoyed very much the jokes that the preachers told on each other and the experiences they had in their different fields. Some of the yarns seem to me to be incredibable; they were certainly very hard ones.

On Sunday evening a Rev. Mr. Burns, I think from New Orleans, preached in the Baptist church one of the most eloquent sermons I have ever heard. It was about the Resurrection, and his flights of oratory were grand. The preachers discussed the sermon, and most of them condemned it. I do not now recollect on what ground, but I thought it was because they could not do anything like as well. The preacher that had preached the introductory sermon before the association and who I thought had made quite a failure was very pronounced in his criticism.

The people were delighted with it, and a delegation waited on Mr.

Nineteenth-century boat traffic on the James River was considerable, and included both workboats and pleasure boats.

Burns and asked that he remain and preach Tuesday night. After the sermon that night Dr. A. B. Brown, then pastor of the church, arose and said he wished to thank the speaker for his sermon and to apologize to him for what he had said about the sermon on Sunday. There were very few if any who had heard that Dr. Brown had said anything against it, yet he said he had done so publicly and now wished to take back all he had said, as he now was sure he was mistaken and done the brother an injustice.

That summer we had quite a number of young ladies visiting my sisters, some of them from King and Queen County, so brother hired quite a large pleasure boat and invited a number of young men and ladies and started to the fort [Monroe] to an outdoor concert of the garrison's band. We did not arrive in time for the music and started on our return about 10. We came becalmed in the [Hampton] Roads and floated about all night. The boat had no oars—in fact was too large to row. That night we witnessed one of the most brilliant meteors I ever saw. It seemed to burst and lighted up all Hampton Roads, it seemed to me for several minutes. We all had a good time, and gave no thought of the anxieties we were causing in Hampton.

We arrived at Hampton wharf just before sunrise, and a number of our friends and relatives were there to receive us. We all saw father on the wharf and expected to get a scolding, but as soon as he heard our greetings and knew we were all safe, he left before we landed! We found our breakfast ready when we got home and then were told how anxious the night had been spent by not only our, but all the families who were represented in our party.

Father did not come where we were, but mother informed us how he had spent the night walking between the house and the wharf. I can now somewhat realize the great strain he went through the night, for not only were all of his children, but also several others that were visiting us that he felt responsible for. He never referred to the trip; he was so thankful we were safe and had enjoyed ourselves that he did not wish to mar our pleasure by referring to his anxiety.

In 1859 I was sent to the University of Virginia. This was my first trip from home without some of the family. I had dreaded the thought of missing so much that I was used to at home; I had been petted and spoilt all my life and had been often told, "You will not get such-and-such things when you go away to school," so I imagined that I should be deprived of all the comforts and most of all (to me) necessities of life. I had never done anything and would not wait on myself if a servant could be called.

I was very agreeably surprised that I got on so well and had as good fare as I did. I was awfully homesick but remained the whole nine months. I enjoyed my first trip up the James River immensely. Quite a few of Cary's boys went with me to the university. I roomed with C. H. Causey on West Range. We stopped at the Columbian Hotel in Richmond as our former military instructor, Massenburg, had a position there. He took us about the town to show us the sights.

Dr. A. B. Brown had now charge of the Charlottesville Baptist church, and we were all fond of him—I particularly, as he had been quite intimate at our house in Hampton. I greatly admired him as a man and honored him for his great learning. He was the brightest and most entertaining man I was ever intimate with, and yet so simple, kind, and sympathetic that he endeared himself to all who knew him well. He often came up and had meals with us at the university, and also invited us to his home. We often attended his church, though he usually was too deep and metaphysical to suit most persons. This session I also heard Dr. Alexander Campbell preach. I remember not understanding his sermon—I think he was trying to explain the difference between the soul and the spirit, and he got beyond my depth. He seemed to be a very impressive speaker and a deep thinker.

Now Bishop [John C.] Granberry was then the chaplain and a very fine preacher. I enjoyed very much the Sunday morning lectures on the bible by Professor William H. McGuffey but did not get there very often as they were quite early in the morning. I made the mistake of taking too many studies and too high classes; senior Greek, math, and Latin. I had to study very hard, and though I kept up in my classes and stood fairly well, yet I felt I was not fully prepared for them. Math was my favorite study always, and I made it but failed on the other two. Although I had never tasted liquor of any kind in my recollection, yet to get some of the Hampton boys to join who did occasionally drink, all of us joined "The Sons of Temperance." This is the only secret society I ever belonged to.

The family had moved back to the country [to Newport News farm], as I was away and Sue was going to Chesapeake Female College, now the main building of the Soldiers Home [at Hampton] and boarded with my sister, Mrs. Marrow, who lived in Hampton, and all the others having left school. We all spent a most delightful summer in 1860, the young people visiting each other's houses every day so it was a continual round of enjoyment. The steamship *Great Eastern* was exhibited in Hampton Roads, and crowds from Baltimore, Norfolk, Richmond and surrounding sections visited her daily. We made up a party and spent a day on her; she was truly a great show, though now, being compared with the large schooners and steamers that enter the roads, she would not look so large.

Six of our steamboats could then lay on one side of her, and the then New York steamers looked very small from her deck. She was only very plainly furnished, and the only attraction was her immense size. Her very large freight compartments were truly a wonder to me.

Having with us quite a large party, we spent a very pleasant day and met a good many friends from other places. The officers and crew did not try to add to our enjoyment but seemed to look upon the visitors more in the light of intruders than guests and were totally lacking in common politeness and civility, although the boat was on exhibition and a charge of $1 or 50¢ was made to go aboard.

This summer (1860) Mrs. Marrow lost her youngest daughter, who was about a year old. This was the first death in the family since the death of my sister in 1844, and her death cast a gloom over the whole household for some time.

That fall in going through Richmond, we stopped at the St. Charles [Hotel] where Massenburg was then. Henry Causey not returning and Willie Peek having graduated in medicine, I roomed with George M.

The steamer **Glen Cove,** *1861.*

Peek, still on West Range but nearer Dawson's Row [at the University of Virginia.]

After the election of Lincoln in November there was so much talk of war that there was not much studying, even by those who were usually studious. I tried to study, for I realized that it was my duty. I knew father was anxious to give me all the advantages possible and had and was still denying himself and working hard to supply the means necessary. I found it more and more difficult to draw the mind from what was occurring and center it upon my books. Of course, a good many students did not even try to study, and these interfered with those who tried.

Peek and I came home Christmas; and from Richmond went to West Point, Virginia, as there was a boat running from West Point to Norfolk. This was our first trip on the York River, and as the day was fine we enjoyed the trip immensely, our pleasure only marred by our impatience to reach home. We arrived at the fort at Old Point about 3 o'clock and were met by a carriage to take me home to the country (Newport News). Dinner was waiting for me, and I am sure I did full justice to Aunt Lucy's cooking, if no one else did. I look back to this week as perhaps the happiest I ever spent, though I had no doubt as happy a life as most people who have lived as long as I have.

Though the times were threatening and the political clouds black and gloomy, and though there was also talk of war, yet in our home all was joy, peace, and happiness, and we gave up ourselves to the pleasure of the season. Forgetting all things save the present, we were entirely engrossed in the continual round of gaieties and amusements of the neighborhood. We gave no thought to the impending storm, which was about to come upon us and to forever change all the conditions of our social life. A merciful providence hides the future from us.

On my return [to Charlottesville] I again tried to apply myself to study, but the stirring events increased: the secession of the states in rapid succession, the formation of the Confederate government, the inauguration of Lincoln, our State Convention—they kept us in a continual turmoil. There was little difference of opinion among us; whether we were Whigs or Democrats, all wanted the State to secede and criticized severely all the so-called Union men in the Convention. After the state seceded, on April 17, 1861, Peek and I determined to return home. The rest of the Hampton boys remained, but a majority of the students left. We left the very last of April, I think the 28th or 29th. We came down the James River in the steamer *Glen Cove*, Captain [John H.] Freeman, and soon found out there was a probability of the boat not reaching Norfolk, as there were rumors in Richmond that the river would be blockaded that day by a gunboat. We expected to land at our wharf at Newport News and hoped that the captain could land us, even if he could not get to Norfolk.

When we got down to Burwell's Bay, everyone was on the lookout for the gunboat, and before we got to the mouth of Pagan Creek the smoke of a steamer was seen near Newport News Point, about where the lighthouse now is [at Middle Ground]. We continued on till the captain made it out as a gunboat, but it did not come up the river and we hoped the captain would risk landing us at the wharf, which was nearly two miles this side of where the gunboat lay. He told us he would not run the risk, nor would he run down near enough to signal an English bark that was anchored nearby, a mile above the wharf. The captain of the bark was aboard and told the captain he would put us ashore if we would run near enough to have his yawl take us off. He determined when he found the river blockaded to return to Richmond.

Some six or eight of us landed at the [Carter's] Grove wharf and hired a wood wagon to take us to Williamsburg, seven miles distant. With our trunks for seats, and with only a few loose boards for the bottom of the wagon, we started over the rough country road. There were two ladies along, and we had quite a pleasant time and enjoyed the novel ride, though there was some danger of being pitched out or falling through the bottom. We got to Williamsburg to a late supper at the old tavern. The next morning four of us hired a private carriage

The Federal gunboat **Harriet Lane** *was built as a U.S. Revenue Cutter in 1858.*

to take us to Hampton. We left our trunks to be sent by wagon. Had I left them to be stored, I should have saved all my school books instead of losing every one.

We left at 8 a.m. and arrived at noon and found Hampton much excited, the mails being cut off by the blockade. But after getting home and hearing little news, with time employed in visiting the neighbors, and farming going on as usual, I soon quieted down and did not realize the state of affairs, and in fact knew little that was going on.

The fourth Thursday in May 1861 was election day and was also to ratify by popular vote the Act of Secession passed by the [Virginia] Convention. Brother and I went to Hampton in the morning, though there had been rumors that the Federal authorities would interfere in the election. But we found the town comparatively quiet. We then drove out to New Market, our voting place, where I cast my first vote, for secession and a Democrat. On our way home late in the afternoon we were overtaken by someone who informed us that General Northcott Phelps had marched into Hampton with some soldiers but had informed the citizens that they would not be molested unless there was some overt act. He had been stationed at Old Point some years before and was known to a good many people. He was now a colonel in the [U.S.] voluntary service, commanding a regiment, I think the First of Vermont. This movement had created much excitement, but as they only marched up to the Cross [King and Queen] Street and returned, the people were again quiet, so we did not return but kept on to home.

On the following Sunday we had a great deal of company, both old and young, and in the afternoon the Federal gunboat *Harriet Lane* went up to Seawell's Point and fired on the Confederate battery. All of us young people went down to the mouth of Newport News Creek and witnessed the fight. When we could not see the shot from the battery hit the water, we concluded it hit the boat, and would greatly rejoice, but I do not now think the boat was hit or anyone hurt on either side. (I am not sure that this fight did not occur on Sunday before, nor am I sure it was the *Harriet Lane*.)

The Confederates of Hampton had after Thursday [when secession was voted] placed a guard at Mill Creek [between Hampton and Fort Monroe] so as to be informed of any movement from the Fort, and after this fight they sent a squad to patrol the beach at Newport News to see that there was no attempt to land. A good deal of our company remained until bedtime, and Mary Ann Tabb spent the night. The corporal of the (Confederate) guard, after stationing his men, returned to the house to spend the evening with the young ladies.

About 10 a.m. on May 25, 1861, Jeff Crandol, one of the pickets came up much excited and reported the Yankees landing at the mouth of the Newport News Creek. None of us believed it, but all the young men returned with him but saw no indications that anyone had landed, and we accused Jeff of being afraid and adopting this means to get someone to stay with him. I have never known whether or not any boats came up to reconnoitre, but it is generally believed now that they did.

This was the last happy day spent in our pleasant home and how happy we were in the enjoyment of the present, with not a thought of the future. A good and wise Being keeps the future from us. Could we have looked at what we had to undergo for four or five years, I do not believe one of us could have passed through it alive, but the privations, anxieties, heartaches, and shocks came one at a time. His grace was sufficient to sustain us as they came, and we were often buoyed up with the hope of a speedy termination of hostilities and return to where our home was. Our sensibilities were also no doubt blunted by the exciting and stirring scenes that were daily passing through.

How changed everything was on our return, not only in our own but in the homes of all our neighbors! How many never returned, some buried in unknown graves. A good many of the houses gone, the fields uncultivated and covered with shrubbery, fences burned, orchards destroyed, and everything laid waste.

THE HAILSTORM and hurricane of 1857 which West recalls inflicted great damage on Elizabeth City County. In a low-lying area near Back River, foxes were said to have sought high ground on a slight rise behind the later Francis Asbury School, giving rise to the name "Fox Hill," which persists.

Alexander Campbell, whose sermon impressed West during his first year at the University of Virginia, was a founder of the Disciples of Christ, or Campbellite denomination, an offshoot of the Presbyterian Church, which from 1813 to 1820 was joined to the Baptists but thereafter became another denomination.

William Holmes McGuffey, who taught at the University of Virginia from 1845 to 1873, was author of the *McGuffey Eclectic Readers*, widely used in schools of the period.

The Chesapeake Female College building which fronted Hampton Roads between Old Point and Hampton, became part of the National Soldiers Home in 1870 and was torn down about 1913. The Soldiers Home is today the Hampton Veterans' Administration Center.

The *Great Eastern*, the British ship which visited Hampton Roads in 1860, was the largest steamship to be built until the *Lusitania* was commissioned in 1906. She was 679½ feet long and equipped with propeller, sidewheels, and sails on seven masts. She anchored off Old Point. She was used to lay the Atlantic cable in 1866 and scrapped in 1888.

Mrs. Marrow, whose daughter died in 1860, was West's sister, Mary Emily, married to William P. Marrow of Hampton. In the Victorian style of his day, West referred to them in writing as "Mrs. Marrow" and "Mr. Marrow."

William Peek, who became a physician, and George Peek, an attorney, were Hampton contemporaries of George Ben West and members of a prominent family.

The election of Abraham Lincoln in November of 1860 created apprehension in Virginia and other Southern states because of his antislavery views. The organization of Southern military units was strengthened, looking towards a conflict.

Although a dirt road linked Hampton, Yorktown, and Williamsburg with Richmond, most Peninsulans in West's day travelled by steamers on the James or York Rivers. The York steamer went upriver as far as West Point, compelling the traveler to go overland from that point to Richmond.

Aunt Lucy was a Negro house servant of the West family. She later accompanied the Wests from Newport News to Richmond when the family fled.

Burwell's Bay, on the James River opposite Newport News, is formed by an indentation in the shoreline of Isle of Wight County.

After Virginia seceded from the Union on April 17, 1861, Federal vessels blockaded Hampton Roads, halting all shipping. This prevented delivery of mail by ship to Hampton, Newport News Point, and other sites formerly served by vessels.

The "old tavern" where West and his University of Virginia companions stopped in Williamsburg en route home to the Peninsula in April, 1861, could be any of nearly two dozen hostelries then operating there. The most famous Williamsburg tavern, the Raleigh, had burned in 1859.

The area of Elizabeth City County around Mill Creek, which separated Old Point Comfort from Hampton, was guarded by Confederates in the early days of the war to prevent Federal infiltration from Fort Monroe into the adjoining Peninsula.

The Wythe Rifles, home defense force of the lower Peninsula, was under Colonel Benjamin Ewell, CSA, a West Point graduate who was president of William and Mary. Major John B. Cary, CSA, George Ben West's former teacher, commanded the Hampton unit of the Wythe Rifles.

Preliminary reconnaissance of Newport News was made by a small force on May 25, 1861, under Major General Benjamin Butler.

He wrote:

> We landed at a little jetty at Newport News and climbed the banks. Here there burst upon my sight one of the finest scenes I ever beheld. At the point nearest the river was a farmer's house [Parker West's] shaded by some very fine elms, and a field of some sixty or seventy acres, a perfect plain, covered with a beautiful growth of spring wheat waving in a light wind.

When it was clear the Federal conquest of Hampton was inevitable, Colonel John Bankhead Magruder, CSA, on August 7, 1861, gave orders for his troops to burn Hampton. Immediately after May 23, 1861, when General Butler refused to return three runaway slaves belonging to Colonel Charles K. Mallory of Hampton, other ex-slaves came in great numbers, establishing the contraband camps. By July 30 at least 1,000 contrabands were encamped in the Hampton-Fort Monroe area, and these had increased to 1,500 the following March. After Lincoln's Emancipation Proclamation on January 1, 1863, soldiers and gunboats which raided plantations up the James would routinely carry former slaves to Fort Monroe, where they lived in areas known as "Slabtown" and "Scuffletown." In January 1866, a Federal officer estimated that 70,000 blacks had gathered during the war around Hampton, Newport News, Yorktown, and Norfolk.

Coastal guns called Columbiads were sent from Fort Monroe in June 1861 and erected by Union troops at Newport News Point. The scene is from **Leslie's Illustrated News.**

CHAPTER IV

When the Yankees Came

I WILL DESCRIBE WHERE OUR NEIGHBORS LIVED and who they were; it may be of interest hereafter. I will begin on Hampton Roads where Captain Charles Hewins lives. His house is in the yard of Mr. George M. Bates, who had two sons and a wife, the young men's stepmother. He and his wife died in Richmond, as did Mallory Bates, the oldest son, who was married and lived some distance from the [Hampton] Roads, back of his father's. Quincy, the youngest, returned, but neither his father's or brother's house nor any outhouses were left. Mrs. Mallory Bates married and never returned. Mr. Celey Smith lived at what is called Blackmore's with his wife and two grown sons. All of his daughters were married. Only the oldest boy returned to the land; no house was on it.

Across Salter's Creek was the Burk farm, which had been bought by father and on which lived my brother William, near [the later] Chesapeake Avenue and Twelfth Street. He died in Richmond in 1862, and not a sign of a house remained when the war ended. Mr. Ned Parrish lived in the house now occupied by Pulliam, near Chesapeake Avenue and Tenth Street. His only son and Mrs. Quincy Bates had died a year or more before. His family consisted of himself and wife and her mother, Mrs. Williams; his youngest daughter, Mat; and E. T. Ivy, son of his oldest daughter; and Mattie Bates, a grandchild. The father, mother, and grandmother died in Richmond, and Mat returned with her nephew and niece just before the war closed. The houses were standing, having been saved by their negroes' occupying them. Mat did not get possession till after the war.

Uncle Jack Parrish lived in the old house back of the Taylor house, with his wife; they had lost all their children young. He did not leave

This map from Harper's Magazine *of spring, 1861, shows Fort Monroe (facing page, center), counterclockwise to the City of Hampton, Hampton Creek and Newport News Point, all located across the Hampton Roads waterway, filled with ships, from Norfolk (this page, top left) and the Elizabeth River.*

home but died during the war, and his wife moved to a relative's in York County and died soon after the war. Father lived, according to the Old Dominion Land Company map, on Washington Avenue extended, near Eleventh Street. Brother and mother died during the war, and not a vestige of house, or outhouses, or orchards remained, and the spot could be only located by some locust trees sprung from stumps. It had been enclosed by the prison (of war) camp established in April 1865 by the Federals. The storehouse father built in 1860 at the foot of Seventeenth Street, according to the map above-mentioned but on Eighteenth Street according to the city map, was occupied by Alex Wood, who was killed. The house on the bluff above our storehouse and now occupied by Captain Haughton as an office, was the residence of Mr. George Merriam, who had recently married. He died also during the war.

Captain [William Jones] Wilbern with his daughter, Mrs. Face, her child Ida, and his granddaughter, Ann Wilbern, lived in Twenty-seventh Street on the bluff. They were caught in the [Federal] lines and did not leave. The Hawkins house is still standing at Thirty-fifth Street near the James River. Mr. John Hawkins lost his wife in 1860. His daughter Indie, and son Richard and nephew William lived with him. William, being a cripple, did not leave home but died before the end of the war. The others returned. Mr. Robert Lee, wife, and some small children lived about Forty-second Street near Washington Avenue; a fort was built around his house, and there was no sign of it when the war closed. He went to Norfolk to live. Mrs. Betsey Lee lived about Forty-eighth and Washington; had two daughters married and not living with her, and five sons. All were in the [Confederate] army; one was killed, and she was dead at the end of the war.

Mr. Armistead Haughton and wife and two sons and two daughters lived about Sixtieth Street and Lafayette [Huntington] Avenue. Their house was destroyed and the father and mother died. Mr. William Lee lived with a large family of daughters and one son, and a second wife [west of the present Sixtieth Street]. He died during the war, and there was no trace of the house after the war. Mr. George Melson lived near Twenty-fifth and Jefferson, and remained. Sam Cealey lived on the Casey farm at Thirtieth and Roanoke, but left during the war and the houses were destroyed, and he died. William Ivy left and lost his house on Twenty-second Street and Parrish Avenue. John Williams stayed but had two sons die in the army. One son, John, returned. Charles Jones remained and saved his house, so also the Skinners and Heaths. William Causey and family returned to the farm after the war but without a house.

So one can somewhat see the changes in this neighborhood from the May morning of 1861 to 1865. Very few of the people when they refugeed took all of their slaves, though most of them took a few of their house servants.

On Monday, May 27 (after the Sunday written about) soon after breakfast, several boats were seen loaded with troops going up the river and being so near the land, it was apparent they intended to land at the wharves. One wharf, fathers, was at the foot of now Eighteenth Street, and the other, rented by Merriam and Gill, was at the upper side of Pier 5, and on the beach at the foot of this wharf they had a store. There had been a wharf and storehouse here since about 1851.

I was the only male at the house, father being out in the field attending to his hands. Mr. Marrow, whose wife and child were here, had gone to the Casey farm, a part of which he cultivated, and brother was at his own place, the Burk farm. One can imagine the great excitement produced by the sight of the troops. War seemed to have come in the midst of perfect peace. I went at once in search of father, who was so large and fat and so troubled by rheumatism that he could not walk, but had to attend his farming riding in a carry-all. I met Jeff Crandol, who was still on duty but had left his post on the beach for reasons I never knew, and was returning to it. I informed him of the landing of the troops and told him to report, which he no doubt did, for he at once returned.

Before I reached the bridge that crossed the Newport News creek, I met James Henry Tabb in a buggy to carry his sister home. He continued to the house and fortunately returned and crossed the bridge with her before it was picketed by the Yankees. I could not find father, so I returned home. Soon brother came up on horseback, being a member of the cavalry. He had to report and, concluding he would be of no great advantage to us and fearing arrest as a soldier, he forded the creek at its mouth, thinking the soldiers had reached the bridge.

In a short time father came to the house. And Mr. Marrow [the author's brother-in-law], who was a member of the Wythe Rifles, and who had been persuaded by father on Friday to move his furniture from Hampton to Mr. Lewis Davis' near New Market, and bring his family to us, came to get his uniform and rifle. He had walked from the Casey farm, and since all our horses were in the fields at work and the Yankees were by this time all in sight, we did not think he could escape, so he concluded to stay and leave at night.

Very soon after, a squad of marines came to the house and advised father to go and ask protection of the commanding officer, who turned out to be General Phelps. They said many of the soldiers were the roughs and jailbirds of Boston and would steal and destroy everything unless it was guarded. We took their advice, and father and I went over and found the general laying off the entrenchment, afterwards built. This battery extended in a semi-circle from the foot of Pier 2 to Pier 8 or 9, striking Eighteenth Street at Mrs. Wingfield's (Washington Avenue extended), and at this point was built quite a strong earthwork on which were mounted afterwards some heavy guns. General Phelps was the colonel of the 1st Vermont (Regiment), but on account of his West Point training had been made brigadier general, though the Massachusetts colonel was his senior in point of service.

There were three regiments landed: the 7th New York, all Germans, were stationed next to our house, all on our land; the 1st Vermont; and the Massachusetts, next to Captain Wilbern's.

We found the General in the center of the camp, and as soon as the request was made and the house pointed out, he turned to a corporal and said "Take three men and go with Mr. West and guard his property and do as he tells you." They returned with us, and up to this time only the Marines had been to the house. Our yard enclosed all the outhouses, barns, stables, and all, and the fence was made of horizontal plank. A partition fence separated the barn from the house yard. I wished the corporal to place the guard on the outside of the fence, and thus they could keep anyone from the rear of the houses, but he was a timid fellow and as the guards would not be in sight of each other this way, he placed them inside of the fence, and the beats were in front of the houses instead of the rear.

The negroes in the fields had, on the landing, gone to their quarters and left the horses and mules in the field. The quarters were near the bridge (over Newport News Creek), and Mr. Tom Skinner, our overseer, lived in the house nearby. (He was killed in battle.) Our cook, Aunt Lucy, and her family lived in the kitchen in the yard, but

By late June, 1861, Camp Butler was fully built and the Vermont Regiment was encamped in tents. This image appeared in **Harper's Weekly** *on June 29, 1861.*

her two boys, who were in the field, went to the quarters and we did not see them again.

As the soldiers were now walking around, Mr. Marrow and I asked the corporal to go out in the fields with us while we caught the horses. We feared we might be shot by some of the soldiers, who might think we were trying to escape. The corporal evidently thought this a ruse on our part to get away, and was very careful to keep us at a distance and always in his front. We after awhile caught all the horses and put them in the stables.

In the excitement of the morning, the family, fearing to have the rifle and uniform belonging to Marrow in the house should the house be searched, had gotten Aunt Lucy to put them under our smoke-house, which was on low pillars, with the rear exposed to anyone who should look under. When we began to realize this and that Aunt Lucy or her daughters might tell some soldiers, it became a question how to get them out unobserved by anyone on guard, for we were sure that if found they [the Federal soldiers] would accuse Mr. Marrow as the owner, for the uniform was too small for me, and of course, we believed he would be at once imprisoned.

We had dinner cooked for the guard, and as all the other soldiers had gone to camp to dinner, we invited them (the guardsmen) to go to the front porch to eat. We also got all the negroes out of sight, and then I took the bundle and rifle and carried them to the barn and hid them in a large pile of oats. In the afternoon we feared that the oats might be taken to feed any horses that they might have, and as things became quiet and we did not fear so much that the house would be searched, we concluded it was better to have them in the house. We had no difficulty in getting the guard to their supper on the porch, and I brought them (uniform and rifle) back to the house. I do not know where they were kept, but they were sewed up in a bed when we moved away and thus saved.

We were all anxious during our stay for fear that Mr. Marrow would be arrested. The negroes informed the soldiers that he was a volunteer, and several times he was accused by them, but whether or not Phelps knew it we never knew. Marrow kept as much as possible from all intercourse with the guards or any other soldiers. This had been a very exciting and fatiguing day to us all, yet we feared to go to bed, but what sleep we got was lying down in our clothes while other watched. We early put out all the lights in the house and watched from the windows the campfires and the guard in the yard. Some of us were going from one window to another all night long. Whether so ordered or not, the guard kept their beat around the house instead of the premises. I think they feared that Marrow and I might escape. The long dismal night passed, but we dreaded the day; we did not know what it would bring but we feared every imaginable thing.

The guards of Vermonters proved to be efficient and reliable and considerate. They were most country lads and felt for our situation. They allowed no soldiers in the yard, but numbers of them came to the fence. In order to conciliate the guard, we furnished them with food, but they were very suspicious, and I usually had to eat some of it to show that it was not poisoned. They would say "We have plenty to eat and do not need anything," but after I would eat some, they seemed to enjoy it. Father did not go over to the camp on business again, but when we wished any information or favors I would write a letter in father's name and take one of the guards as a protection, and have the interview with the general. I am glad to record that I was always received by him as well as his adjutant with the utmost courtesy and consideration, and the requests were always granted in a kind and cordial manner. They seemed to realize the embarrassing and unfortunate position in which the family was placed and did all they could to help us and make our stay as pleasant as possible.

I could hardly believe that General Phelps had been harsh and unkind to the people of Louisiana in 1862, when the papers accused him of it, or that the adjutant within ten days after their landing should set fire to Colonel Mallory's house on the Sawyer Swamp Road above New Market. It was a rumor that Phelps had resigned in the army on account of insanity; his eyes certainly looked wild, but to me he always showed the utmost kindness and granted every request made of him.

Tuesday afternoon late I went over to the camp to request permission for father and me to go out the lines to see after his other property and find out what our neighbors were doing or intended to do. The pass was given me for the next day. While in camp I witnessed something of what war is. It was a sad sight to me, for I did not know what it meant and imagined it worse than it was. It seemed that the colonel of the Massachusetts Regiment was very mad because Phelps had been promoted over him and for this reason perhaps had given passes to a great many of his men to go out of the lines—or perhaps the soldiers having just entered the service did not ask for passes. At any rate, a large number had gone out of camp and plundered the whole neighborhood.

Phelps had instructed the pickets to arrest all without passes or having any kind of stolen goods. There were a hundred or more around headquarters having every kind of household goods, and some with carts loaded with plunder. I did not know then that the neighbors had left their homes and that most of the plunder was from deserted houses, but I thought it had been taken from the people and imagined all sort of cruel treatment to our friends. They seemed to have stripped the farms and houses of everything conceivable. I learned afterwards that the thieves, finding out they would be arrested, had left most of the plunder in the thickets outside of the pickets, all of which was afterwards brought into camp, in the night.

As only two of the Vermonters were arrested, and very few of the Germans, the Massachusetts Regiment became very indignant and made many threats. I now saw what a soldier would do if unrestrained and in what he conceived an enemy's country. We learned the next day that what was taken had been left by our friends who had fled from their homes and were able to carry only a little more than their clothes. I never knew whether any punishment was inflicted, but there was a fear of mutiny, for we were informed by our guard that the Vermont Regiment was expecting an attack, and if we heard any firing we would know it was between them and the Massachusetts Regiment. If our troops had but known this, how easily it would have been to start them to fighting.

How could we sleep, fearing as well as hoping that a battle would take place in the camp? So again we did not undress, but watched at the windows all night, and at the least noise those who were sleeping would be aroused. Thus we spent another long and dreary night, filled with uncertainty and anxiety.

While at camp Tuesday, General Phelps informed me that the German regiment were complaining that the Vermont guard had to pass their lines to and from our house, and he would have to take the guard in future from the German regiment. I was very unwilling for the change, not only because we could not understand them, but I was sure they would not prove as efficient soldiers. Phelps said they would do what they were told, but if on trial they did not prove satisfactory, he would remove them and station his own men.

Wednesday morning a German guard was sent and the same instructions given—not to allow a soldier to come in the yard. After breakfast father and I went out to visit the neighborhood and first went to George Melson's, who told us that many of our neighbors had left their homes on Monday and left everything behind. He walked with me, father riding, and we next went to Samuel Cealey's, at the Casey farm. He and his family were at home, but were doing nothing but trying to keep what they had from strolling soldiers. They afterwards moved, and the houses were destroyed by the Yankees. The negroes were at the Casey house but doing no work and were in a state of great excitement and jollification; but they were polite and respectful and did not have an idea of what was to be done.

We then went to brother's place [Burk farm] and were told by the negroes that he had left Monday and had not been seen since. The negroes had not tried to protect anything from the pillaging of the soldiers the day before. What furniture or other things they wanted had been carried away by them. A small iron safe that father had used in his store in Hampton had been brought out by brother, and it contained all his and father's books and papers and some jewelry belonging to Mrs. Marrow and Aunt Eliza Tabb. It had been taken out in the yard and broken open. The valuables were all stolen and books and papers scattered about the yard. I picked up the books and many papers but do not think anything proved to be of any value.

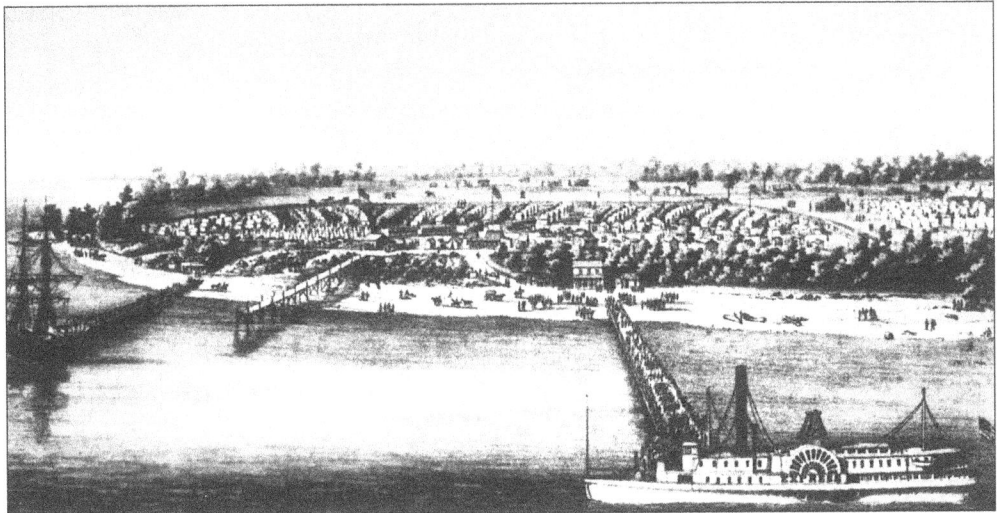

Camp Butler at Newport News had grown to these proportions when this lithograph of it was published in Baltimore late in 1861. The West farm would be located at the far right, but is not depicted here.

THE TRACTS OF LAND West described in this chapter encompass most of the lower Peninsula from the present Indian River Creek (formerly Bates' Creek) in Hampton to the present Huntington Park in Newport News. Careful study of this portion of the West memoirs was made in the 1930s by the late William Tilden Stauffer, Newport News attorney, who published his findings in *The William and Mary Quarterly*, the *Newport News Daily Press*, and in *Newport News' 325 Years*, a 352-page history edited by Alexander Crosby Brown and published in 1946 on the 50th anniversary of the city's charter. In Mr. Stauffer's essay in the latter, he wrote: "The territory now covered by the City naturally divides itself into three sections: the Gookin tract along James River; East End between Newport News Creek (now known as the Boat Harbor) and Salter's Creek; and Celey's (plantation), east of Salter's Creek." In his account of Newport News' early years, Mr. Stauffer quoted extensively from the West memoirs.

Names of many early property owners are perpetuated in Newport News today, including West Avenue, Parrish Avenue, Ivy Avenue, Haughton Lane, and Mallicotte Lane. However, a number of Newport News area landowners died during the Civil War or lost their property during Reconstruction.

Two wharves extended into the James River from Parker West's Newport News farm in 1861 when the war began. One, rented by Washington Burk to Merriam and Gill, who operated a store and dockside post office, was near the present site of Seventeenth Street. The other, operated by West himself, was at the foot of Eighteenth Street. Both are shown in drawings of the Federal invasion in 1861, reproduced in *Harper's Weekly*.

Charles K. Mallory (1820-1875), a member of a distinguished Elizabeth City County family, served as attorney for Parker West and was living on Sawyer's Swamp Road (now Big Bethel Road) in Elizabeth City County when the war came. Born in Norfolk, he studied law at William and Mary and was a member of the Virginia Convention of 1861 which declared for secession. After serving as a Confederate officer, he returned to the practice of law in Hampton. Mallory Avenue there was named for him.

CHAPTER V

So Much Destruction

HOW SAD IT MUST HAVE BEEN TO FATHER TO see so much destruction of what it had required him so many years to accumulate! At Mr. Ned Parrish's we found the negroes in charge and loafing in the yard; all the family had left Monday night, carrying very little with them. The negroes who remained had plenty to eat, and they soon took possession what was left by their owners and did a little farming during the war. As the tide was low, we concluded to go by the beach to Uncle Jack's (Parrish), having heard from the negroes that he and his wife were still there. As we went out of Mr. Ed Parrish's yard to the river, Mr. [George] Melson detected a dozen soldiers behind the fence with their guns aimed at us, and by stopping and going to them he perhaps saved our lives, for they said they thought we were trying to escape by a boat at the landing. They were Germans, and as only one of them could talk any English and he very little, we did not find out what they had been sent out of camp for. We showed our pass, and whether they knew what it was or not, they did not stop us.

When we got to Uncle Jack's we found both in the yard and house a good many soldiers—none of them armed. Mr. Parrish was very excited, and Mrs. Parrish very much distressed and alarmed for fear her husband, though very old, would do some violence, and that his mind would become more unbalanced than it was. (His mind had at times given way, but he had never been at all violent, as far as I know.) They did not know how to rid the house of soldiers, and feared to order them out. Mrs. Parrish said they had some money and had concluded to remain, for they thought they had some knowledge of war, having passed through the War of 1812. He hoped to save his property till the war was over, for none of us believed it would last more than a few months. We told them we would try to have a guard sent to protect them from the strolling soldiers.

When I next saw General Phelps I reported their [the Parrishes'] helpless condition to him and asked him to send them a guard. I do not know whether or not one was ever sent, but if it was, it was continued for only a very short time. As they had no living children, they always kept two or three negro children about the house and petted them like they would their own, though they were not treated as equals. At this time they were particularly fond of a boy now perhaps 16 or 18 who had been in the house since a very little child. He was a bright boy and seemed very fond and considerate of them. This mulatto, though he had been raised almost like a son, was so ungrateful as not long after to break into the house with others and take all the money that this old couple had. The young rascal went off, and neither I nor anyone about here ever knew what became of him. I never saw Uncle Jack and Aunt Lucy again.

Melson stopped at his home, and when we returned early in the evening we found that our yard was full of the German soldiers, some on the porch, and one had even entered the house. The guard could not talk English, and we could not make them understand anything. In fact, all they did was to keep their beats but prevented no one doing what he pleased. I wrote a letter in father's name, complaining of the guard and asking for a guard from the Vermonters, and also informing the General of the fact the negroes would not work, either on our or the neighboring farms; that many were in the camp; and asking his permission to leave with all the family and such negroes who would willingly go with us.

In the expectation of getting permission to leave, Mr. Marrow had been at work all day getting the vehicles and harness together, and putting them in order. Had he not been with us, we should have been minus several carts and would therefore have been able to carry away much less than we did, though we took very little. The weather had been very hot and dry and was still so, and all the tires [steel rims] on the wheels were loose and required much wedging, which I could not have done.

I could get not one of the guard to go with me to camp to carry this letter, so I went with a German who could speak English, for I liked to be accompanied by a soldier for protection and non-interference. But this fellow carried me by the guardhouse of the German regiment and turned me over to the guard. I told the guard that I had the letter for

General Phelps, and they tried to induce me to give it up so they could deliver it. After awhile I demanded to see their colonel and was taken to him, and he also tried to secure the letter, but finding he could not get it, sent me under a guard.

I have always believed the whole regiment had some scheme on hand to do some pillaging at our home, and thought the letter contained charges against the guard, as it did; and that General Phelps would relieve them, as he did. The General was out of his tent, and I was turned over to the adjutant, who was told that I was a suspicious character and perhaps a spy. He was much amused, but I felt very mad and indignant. When the General came back, he readily agreed to let us leave and said he would furnish us a guard, which should be instructed to go with us as far as we wished; and that we could take not only the negroes who were willing to go, but that he would give us the guard to carry those who did not wish to go.

I told him that with the family we could not be bothered with those who would not go willingly. He said, "Then, when you get your family in the Confederate lines, you come back and I will send all your negroes with you." I asked him for a pass to return, but he said it would be unnecessary as I would be brought to him by his pickets if I came back. I then fully intended to return and get the negroes. He denied that any of our or anyone else's slaves were in his camp, or any other kind of property. I had seen in my tramp under guard that several negroes were lounging about the tents, and so informed him. He then insisted that I go through the camp with his orderly and report all I found. I was very unwilling to do so, but he overruled all my excuses and I started, intending to make a very careless investigation, though he told me to go into any tent I wished, and so instructed the orderly.

We had gotten to the line between the Vermont and Massachusetts Regiments when the guard stopped us and said we could not pass. The orderly, who felt his importance as an orderly of the commanding officer, was very indignant, but the cockeyed sentinel refused and called his corporal and officer-of-the-day. I had nothing to say and was glad of the stop and hoped this would end my inspection, but we returned to headquarters and were given such authority that we were not interrupted again.

It must have been suspected why I was going through the camp, for I only saw one negro, and he was at Merriam's store. I did not go

When the August 31, 1861 **Harper's Weekly** *reported on the burning of the town of Hampton by Magruder's rebels, this engraving accompanied the story.*

through the German camp. I reported that I had seen but one negro, but I still believed there were others. I also reported that my brother's buggy was in front of the tent of the Massachusetts colonel, and Phelps said it should be returned to me. He said he realized that we would be subject to many inconveniences if our family remained but that he would do all in his power to assist us and make our stay as pleasant as possible and would protect us and all our property if we remained, yet he thought it best that we leave.

The adjutant told me privately that he commended us for going with our State, and if Vermont had seceded he would have been with her, for he owed his allegiance to his State. The General said he would relieve the guard at night and send again the Vermonters, and also a squad of them next morning to accompany us out of his lines. I never saw him again, but I have always been grateful for his many kindnesses to us and his readiness to comply with all our requests.

When the relief guard came, the Germans refused to let them come to the yard, and at one time I thought there would certainly be a fight, for the Germans threatened to shoot, and the officer-of-the-day placed his men behind a straw rick a short way down the lane and then held a parley. He finally convinced them of his authority and took them [the relief guard] away and left the Vermonters.

We called in Aunt Lucy and her daughters and told them we were going away the next morning, and asked if they wished to go or stay. They had been performing all the duties of their position ever since the landing of the Yankees, and had not had any intercourse with the other negroes, as far as we knew; though we suspected that at least Lucy's two boys, Bill and Henry, came at night, which they could easily do, as the back door of the kitchen opened in the garden.

Father had purchased Aunt Lucy in Mathews County about 1842. She had then a daughter, Hannah, and sons, Bill and John. Father had bought her for a cook, and she proved a most excellent one. Hannah had been made a house servant and proved a most reliable and honest one. Bill, who died during the war, also proved an honest and reliable boy and man, and was a sort of head man on the farm at this time. John was a trifling, exciteable, bad boy, and about 1856 had run away and sent father word he wished to be sold and would never be any account to him unless he was sold, as he wished to go away. After a year or two of trouble with him, father exchanged him for a man, and he was taken south, and we never heard of him again.

Aunt Lucy's husband had been bought by Mr. Joe Segar at the time she was sold, and now they had other children, namely: Henry, about 16, Fanny, about 14, and Cindie, about 10. Her husband had died a few years before, and she had recently married an old man named Jim. Hannah had a daughter about 9 named Henrietta, and one about a year old. Aunt Lucy and her daughters and granddaughters wished to go with us, and we told them to pack their clothes, as we wished to make as early a start as possible in the morning.

We were all very busy till late, packing up the things we thought we would be able to take, and we left behind a great many things packed that we could not carry. But, as I expected to return and get what was left, we thought it did not make so much difference if things were left. We were very late getting to bed, for we had to select such things as we at once should need, for we had very few vehicles. We rested more and better this night than any since the landing. Mr. Marrow and I had to feed up and hitch and pack everything, so we got up quite early and had our breakfast and were ready to start about 9 o'clock.

One cart was loaded with bacon, the others with trunks and bed clothes, some crockery; not a book or single piece of furniture except a common skeleton lounge for father to sleep on was taken. The negroes' clothes were not as well packed and therefore took up much valuable room, though of no intrinsic value. In fact, they took a cart to carry them, for Aunt Lucy insisted upon carrying all the old clothes of her husband. He was one of the old-time negroes who never threw away or gave away old clothes but would put on patches upon patches till it was impossible to tell the original color or piece of cloth, and put to shame Joseph's coat of many colors. They were not only very picturesque but very heavy, thick, and warm.

No persuasion could induce her to leave a single piece behind, though the whole lot would not have brought a dollar, and by carrying these we had to leave some valuable things which we afterwards much needed. But she was persuaded in her mind that he would follow her, and she could not bear the thought of telling him she had left his clothes behind. These clothes to her were as valuable as the best dress suits would have been to people of means, and she carried them around with her during the war and brought them back with her to Hampton after the war, to find that Jim had not been as faithful to her but had married a much younger wife. But be it recorded to his credit that he left his young wife for the one who had been so faithful to his interest and lived as her husband till his death.

Father drove one of the carts; the others were driven by my sisters and the negroes. We had only one single carriage. Sister Mary drove this, and in it were Mammy Watson and mother, with Bettie [his niece, Bettie Marrow], and Hannah's baby. The corporal and his guard came over early to accompany us, and father was very impatient to leave and was at the head of the procession. He had borne up during all this time in a remarkable manner, for he saw that nearly all that he had accumulated in a life of hard work and indomitable energy was being left and much of it already destroyed and laid waste. He must have thought that he would never again have the comforts that he was leaving; yet by nature he was sanguine, hopeful, and of a happy disposition, full of energy and pluck, and was able to bear his loss in a wonderful manner.

As we were about to start, the adjutant drove up in the buggy, drawn by a lot of soldiers, and said that Phelps and the Massachusetts colonel had had a row about the return, which caused the delay in bringing it. I had no time to think or I might have tied it behind a

This William McIlvaine watercolor from 1862 shows a group of Zouaves standing (far right) amid Hampton's ruined buildings, with soldiers and a Union army supply train moving through the background.

cart and thus saved it.

I went in the house to see if any small article of special value had been left and found a double-barrel gun had been overlooked. So as to hide it from the guard, I took down a curtain and, taking the gun apart, wrapped it up and placed it in the carriage. I saw one thing I was glad to leave behind. This was a handsome old clock with wooden wheels which had a way of occasionally striking when it did not run, and some of the family thought when it did so it was the sign of a death in the family—either near or remote family—and of course this caused a great deal of unnecessary distress and anxiety. This I was glad to leave and am truly glad the Yankees got it, but not anything else.

The last order I gave to the guard we left in the yard was to go after a cow and calf some Germans were driving out of the enclosure, on the beach in front of the house.

Mr. Marrow and I walked, and in fact were kept pretty busy looking after our drivers, who were entirely inexperienced, and in seeing to the tires (rims) not coming off the wheels. We had to pass over the bridge through the Pumpkin Hall tract, and to the main road corner of

Madison and Twenty-fifth Street. Then, by the Melson place to Twenty-eighth Street near Virginia Avenue, and then the old country road that ran somewhat parallel with the [later tracks of the] C&O Railroad.

When we passed [the later site of] the railroad Y, we met one of Mr. Hawkins' men, who told us about the Wilberns, Hawkinses, and Lees. He told us also there was a picket of Confederate soldiers at the corner of the Baker Lee road about Thirty-eighth Street, below where the railroad would later be, and told us the names of some who we knew belonged to our cavalry company. I now think this negro lied; at any rate, though the guard had been instructed to go with us till we sent them back and though we were still so near their camp, they became very uneasy, having, I suppose, a prison before their eyes. Though we assured them they would not be imprisoned, yet they said as our men were so near, they thought it unnecessary for them to go with us farther as it might place them and us in an embarrassing position if the picket insisted in taking them to Yorktown, then our [Confederate] headquarters. So we were persuaded to send them back, or rather to let them go back, for we thought if a picket was where the negro said, that they must be only a short distance from our troops.

We had not gotten to the Briarfield road when we met a squad of Germans, I think unarmed. A captain was riding on one of Mr. Hawkins' horses, which seemed to have been taken from a plow, as he still had on the harness. They stopped father, who was some distance ahead, and informed him that he must return, as he evidently was trying to escape. I fortunately had the pass we had used the day before, and when I came up and showed it to the captain, he said that was all right. Though I doubt if he could read it, we were allowed to go on.

When we got to the Briarfield road we looked anxiously for our troops but did not see any sign of them. When we passed Mr. William Lee's, he was near the road superintending six or eight negro men hoeing corn. His family had been sent up to his son-in-law's at Lee Hall. We did not see anyone else attempting any farming. He must have thought that the enemy would not interfere with him or his negroes, and they had evidently not been encouraged to leave their work. In fact, there was at this time no idea of freeing the slaves among the soldiers. I think General Phelps then represented the sentiment of the army—that the negroes were slaves and should be made to work for their owners and returned to them if they left.

THE FEDERAL FORCES landing at Newport News made no effort to seize, lure, or alienate the slaves on Parker West's farm. Accordingly, George Ben West asked the Federal commander, General Phelps, to permit the Wests to take their slaves when they fled the Newport News farm. Permission was granted, and the Wests took their house servants; George Ben West planned to return to the farm later for the field hands. He never did because Federal policy towards slaves was abruptly changed by General Benjamin Butler, USA, who was Phelps' superior in command on the Peninsula. In an 1861 confrontation at Old Point with Confederate officers, who came there to claim three runaway slaves of Charles K. Mallory, Butler declared them contraband of war and thus subject to enemy seizure. Many runaway slaves followed them, and Fort Monroe, Hampton, and nearby Camp Hamilton soon were overrun with ex-slaves, who were put to work by the Union Army. After Lincoln issued the Emancipation Proclamation on January 1,1863, their number increased.

USA Gen. Benjamin F. Butler

At the time the Wests left their Newport News farm in May 1861, the Federal line had advanced only a few miles northwest of Newport News Point. The picket line was patrolled by Federal soldiers, and only Phelps' written pass enabled the Wests to pass into Warwick County, where Confederates were in control, and westward to Williamsburg and Richmond.

West writes that "Sister Mary", or Mrs. William P. Marrow, drove one of their farm wagons, his father drove another, and negro servants the other three. George Ben West and his brother-in-law William Marrow walked, evidently to reduce the loads.

Briarfield Road, which the Wests traversed as they drove west, was then a rural road in Warwick and Elizabeth City counties, and was traversed by soldiers from Newport News en route to the Battle of Bethel.

William Lee, whose house the Wests passed, lived on the James River near Newport News' present Sixty-fourth Street. He was a kinsman of Richard Decautur Lee of Lee Hall, a handsome brick plantation house built in Warwick County in 1848-59 and still standing.

West writes of slaves at work on William Lee's farm in Warwick County, despite the Federal invasion. However, farming in Tidewater declined as Union General George B. McClellan's forces moved up the Peninsula in 1862.

A group of contrabands, standing with an official person, is shown in this pencil drawing by Alfred R. Waud. "Newport News 1861" would have referred to the area where the West farm was located.

CHAPTER VI

We Refugees Were Poor

WE TRAVELLED VERY SLOWLY, AS THE TIRES [STEEL rims] had to be frequently inspected, and where there was any water along the road, we would dip it up and pour it on them. So it was late in the evening before we got to Mr. W. C. Marrow's. He informed us that the house of Mr. J. P. Mallicotte, on the opposite side of the road, was vacant as his family had refugeed. We drove in and took possession and spent the night, but doing a very little unpacking. Mr. Marrow left us to report to his company, which was then at Yorktown. The most exaggerated reports were being made and circulated about the movements and doings of the soldiery. It was reported that all of us had been fearfully treated; that Mr. Marrow and I had been arrested and marched through Hampton naked; that he had been hung and I was to be hung; that my single sisters had followed me and been most shamefully treated; and other rumors as wild and untrue as these, which I have forgotten.

The rumors I suppose were published in the Richmond papers, for [Robert R.] Howison, who wrote a sort of history during the war, I think, in the *[Southern] Literary Messenger,* called attention to the atrocities of the Yankees among others, and mentioned some of these rumors about us, and gave them as facts. (I do not know whether his history came out in a book form or not.) As soon as I learned of the publication, I contradicted it in the *Richmond Dispatch,* but do not know whether or not Howison ever corrected it. We were treated as kind and considerate as it was possible, and I believe everything was done for us that could have been and we had not the least cause for complaint. We were very grateful that we were treated so much better than we expected or feared. I think it was all due to the fact that General Phelps was a gentleman and felt sorry for us in the position in which we were placed. Though

This sketch appeared in **Harper's Weekly** *on June 29, 1861. It depicts a time soon after Hampton was burned when only a few chimneys and part of St. John's Church (far right, rear) were left standing.*

there were many rumors about the Yankees marching up the country, we did not believe them and therefore lay down this Thursday night with less nervous strain and a greater feeling of security than we had since Sunday night.

The carts were left loaded and drawn up close to the house, with a hound dog tied to one of them for a guard. Father was very fond of a pure black-and-tan mother dog we had owned a few years and tried to get her to follow him from home. As she would not follow, I put her in one of the carts, but before we got to the main road she jumped out and returned. When we passed the overseer's house, his hound had followed us. He proved to be a very fine guard dog, and we all became much attached to him, and when in 1862 father moved the family to Lynchburg, he loaned him to a farmer near Richmond, and we never claimed or saw him again.

We went very early to sleep as we all were entirely worn out. I lay out on the porch near the carts and was awakened by the dog's furious attack on someone, and as I arose someone struck the porch with his sword, and I thought the Yankees had us again. Mr. Ivy and Mr. Pompey Marrow had come over to see us, and the dog had broken loose and had been so ferocious that Ivy had drawn his sword to protect himself and had struck the porch instead of the dog. It was quite early in the night. We learned that our outer pickets were then at Persimmon Ponds bridge, a few miles above, so father decided we would go up to Mr. Walls', just inside the outer pickets.

After breakfast we started and met [Colonel, later] General [John Bankhead] Magruder [CSA] near the picket, with some cavalry, reconnoitering. He stopped and enquired as to the number and position of the Yankees—whether they had thrown up entrenchments—and intimating that he would attack them. He seemed to feel very sorry for father and told him to go to Yorktown, and he would furnish us quarters and would supply all our wants as long as he had anything to eat himself. We have always felt very kindly to him for his kindness and offer, and in fact, he was kind to all of the refugees and did all in his power to help them. We found Mr. Walls' family had gone to Williamsburg, and he being at home alone, he put his house and everything else he had to our service. We remained there till Monday.

What a week this had been! I was completely broken down, and all of us were more than half sick. My sickness and the reports about Magruder's going to attack Newport News caused me to give up all idea of going back for the furniture and negroes. I have been surprised at how much I have remembered of the happenings of the three days in the Yankee lines, but these days represent, it seems to me, a long life. The strain on my mind and anxiety was so great that I have often thought that a few more such days would have completely unbalanced my mind. Persons whom I had known only a short time I completely forgot, and no consideration could be offered me to undergo such an experience again—not even if I could become young again.

Father found out that a great many of the refugees were living in Williamsburg and concluded we would go up there, believing the war would be of short duration. We started Monday morning, but in the afternoon a thunderstorm appeared, and we were overtaken by Mr. Richard Lee near his home, Lee Hall, so we stopped there, as Mr. Lee was very pressing in his invitation. The storm proved to be a very severe one, and we remained all night. We rented a house in Williamsburg

Big Bethel, the Peninsula site of an early Civil War skirmish, from Harper's Weekly *of April 26, 1861.*

with uncle Robert Davis and lived in camp style, sleeping on the floors and having very few comforts and no conveniences. With the exception of a few families, the people of Williamsburg seemed to think we were intruders, and they would have to support us. They showed very little sympathy for our condition.

After the battle of [Big] Bethel, June 10, we did not feel so safe in Williamsburg, and brother and father thought it best for us to move to Richmond. I will relate an incident of the morning of the battle, though not connected with our family, yet the Mrs. Hannah Tunnel spoken of had before her marriage with George Tunnel and before we moved to Hampton been an inmate of our family, doing sewing and teaching the older children, and thus we somewhat looked upon her as one of us, and we all loved her and her family. She was a Miss Nicholson, a daughter of a surveyor of Elizabeth City County. She was stopping at Colonel Mallory's place a few miles above New Market bridge, on the Sawyer Swamp Road.

On the morning of the battle, a [Federal] detachment from Newport News and one from Old Point had quite a fight at New Market, on account of the Old Point troops mistaking the troops from Newport News for Confederates. This was very early in the morning and I do not think many were hurt, though the firing lasted some little time. Mrs. Tunnel walked up the road and informed a detachment of [Confederate] cavalry under Major [James Henry] Lane that the Yankees were advancing. Generals Magruder, D. H. Hill, and Lane all give the credit to her for not only saving the advance guard but also in saving the battle of great Bethel. Mrs. Tunnel died in September 1871 and is buried in the Old St. John's Churchyard [Hampton], in an unmarked grave.

Soon after the fight we went out to the farm of Mr. William Burk on the Chickahominy, and remained a day or two. From there, mother, Mammy Watson, Sue, Lizzie, Bettie, and the baby of Hannah, took a steamboat to Richmond, and the rest of us, together with Aunt Liza Tabb and Sheilds, her son, drove up to Richmond. We had to pass one night on the road and expected to spend it at a Colonel Lacy's, to whom we had a letter of introduction, but by mistake we passed Colonel Lacy's, and when we reached the next house it was after sunset. We drove up to the house to ask for accommodations for the night, and on account of our dirty and not very respectable appearance, there was some hesitancy on the part of Mr. Appleton to take us in. But we were soon made at home and treated very kindly by all the family. We did not unpack anything, so I remained in the carriage all night to guard our things.

The next day we passed Bottom's Bridge about noon, and the first house we came to was a small dilapidated one on our right, in a shady yard, so we stopped to eat our dinner and to buy forage for the teams for we did not have any. An old man seemed to be living alone at the place, and everything showed he was very poor. (I have always been sorry that I did not remember his name). He had very little corn or fodder but let us have all we wanted, so we took some with us besides what the horses ate. When we asked him the price, he said he made no charge and was glad to furnish it, and when we insisted on his taking the money (for we saw he was not able to give it) he said to father, "Even if you had an abundance of money, yet I would not take a cent from you under any consideration, as you have had to leave your home and are now casting your lot with the South."

I have often thought of the circumstance and his great kindness and wished I could have had the pleasure of showing him in some way how highly I appreciated his sympathy and kindness. I have often seen how few friends one has when really in the need of them, and this is one of the oases I have found in the desert of life. This was only a small thing, and yet it has made me think better of mankind on account of it, and I still like to think of it and I hope it has made me better and more willing to help others and to sympathize with them. We can never tell the far-reaching effect of a small act of kindness.

That afternoon, the latter part of June '61, we reached Richmond and attracted as much attention and curiosity as an army corps did a year or two after. We were not an attractive sight driving through the city, and I had to often reply to inquiries as to where we were from and why we were moving. I suppose some of them got an idea of what war was. In going up Twenty fifth Street we saw Jim Causey, who took us out to where his father was living on Thirtieth and M Streets. I think had we not seen Jim Causey that father intended to go to Mr. Burk's on Broad and Twenty-third. The next day the rest of the family came up by boat. One can imagine how we had to live with so many people living in a small house.

In a few days we rented a house on Thirty-fourth and P streets from a Mrs. Hill, at $12.50 a month. It was a large two-story brick house, with a large two-story brick kitchen and also a smokehouse and stable. The lot was one-fourth of a square. We kept the house till after the war, and though at the close of the war Confederate money was almost valueless, yet we only paid the $12.50 a month as at first when we were on a gold basis. Soon Mr. Ned Parrish's family rented part of the house and remained till about 1863. We lived as two families, but in the closest kind of intimacy. Mr. Festus Malone and his wife lived across Thirty-fourth Street and were very kind and friendly, and the Brown family, Mrs. Malone's father, mother, and sisters, also lived there. The Causeys soon bought on the same block, and the Schmelz [family of Hampton] lived for some time on an adjoining block, and also the Bates family.

We did not form many intimacies with the Richmond people. We refugees were poor and kept very much to ourselves and visited seldom outside ourselves. Though I believe that all of them would testify to the kind treatment of all the Richmond people, I soon found out that the family would be unable to live or make a living if I should go in the army. I think we moved into the house the last of June. I do not think father had $100 when we left home, and most of this was gone. He could do nothing, and we all decided we would almost starve before we would sell any of the slaves, and none of them could bring much hire. All the family were much opposed to my enlisting, for they believed I could not stand the hardships of camp life. Besides, I was needful to them.

I was fortunate in securing a situation in the Quartermaster Department under Major J. F. Whitfield, through the influence of General Virginius Groner, a very intimate friend of my brother's, he being in the Adjutant General's Office. I went to work for $50 a month on July 1. Father was able soon to sell his horses, mules and carts, and we bought enough furniture for the house and kitchen to make us comfortable. I was employed to have charge of some warehouses on the [James River] basin where were stored the baggage of the soldiers from the South, who had each one left home with trunks and valises, mess chests, etc. As transportation could not be secured beyond Richmond, the [Confederate] government rented these warehouses and stored the baggage. My duty was to deliver to any soldier who was in the city or returning home for any cause, his baggage. It was stored by regiments and it was quite a job to find the luggage in such a large pile of trunks, etc. I remember the 12th Georgia Regiment's baggage was oftenest called for and am quite sure that this regiment had more baggage stored than the whole Army of Northern Virginia had with them in 1864. Very little of it was ever called for, and I suppose was burned in 1865, though I do not know what became of it as I had charge only a few months.

At first I would go to the office in the morning for the keys, and then go to the warehouses and stay around there all day, and often would not have a caller during the whole day. I told the Major I could help in the office and preferred to do so, if he would let me put up notices on the warehouses where I could be found in case I was needed. His business was to furnish feed to the horses of all officers in the city, the cavalry, the artillery, and the teams of the army around the city, so I soon had assigned me the duty of receiving requisitions for forage and giving orders to the different men in charge of the oats, corn, or hay. This was my business during the whole war, and I became so proficient and essential to the department that I was exempt from military duty even on raids, when most everybody, even soldiers on furlough, were obliged to go to the front when the city was threatened.

Whitfield's office was on the southwest corner of Bank and Tenth streets in the second story, and one of the duties of the office was to pay some of the departments, but I have forgotten which. I remember, though, that I several times took money to the staff of President [Jefferson] Davis and thus knew all of them. He also had to buy

On their flight from Newport News, the West family traveled through
Warwick and James City counties to Williamsburg. Warwick Courthouse,
shown here, was then a Confederate post.

stationary for the departments, and I remember an amusing incident in
the purchasing of some ink. The Major was a drinking man; also one of
his clerks, W. O. Smith. One day the Major came in in a hurry and put
down on Smith's desk a bottle of ink in a black bottle similar to some
that whisky comes in, and said "Bill, try this" and went out. Smith,
thinking it whisky, put the bottle to his mouth and took a good swig
before he got the taste of the ink. I expect it was well that Whitfield was
out of hearing. We clerks enjoyed the joke immensely, and so did the
Major when he returned.

Brother, who was a fine penman and bookkeeper, soon found out
the family could not live on the salary I was getting though I was helped
by all the family taking in work, making shirts and pants for the soldiers,
for which they got good prices from the government. Through General
Groner, he got his discharge from the cavalry and got a good position
in the Adjutant General's office that fall. After this we made out very
well, not only to feed but clothe ourselves, for money then was as good
as gold and provisions were not extra high. Mrs. Marrow went down to

Yorktown and through the lines and found much of her furniture that had been taken from Hampton in May and stored at Mr. Lewis Davis'. So that fall and winter we had quite a good time, being all together except Mr. Marrow, and it was seldom that we did not have stopping with us some of the Peninsula soldiers. Mr. Parrish was passionately fond of dominoes and every night we went up in his room and had games of dominoes. Aunt Eliza [Tabb] and Sheilds went to Norfolk to live with George S. West, who had been discharged from the army on account of his health.

Our armies had for the most part been victorious in every engagement, and our friends had for the most part not done much fighting, and so none were killed or wounded and we were sure the war would soon be over. Therefore we gave ourselves up to all the enjoyment possible under the circumstances. I have no recollection of how we spent the next Christmas [1861] but am pretty sure we had quite a pleasant time, considering it was war times.

I went to the office a little before 9 o'clock and remained till about 6. The first year I took dinner at a restaurant or boarding house, but as money began to depreciate and things became higher, we had to economize more and more, and then I would take a small snack in my pocket to eat in the middle of the day. At home they did not have dinner, but waited till brother and I got home in the evening. We raised our vegetables in our gardens. I worked in the office as much Sunday as any other day. The first and last of the month for four or five days I was kept very busy, but the balance of the time had not a great deal of work to do, but had always to be present in the office in case anyone came in for forage. In the spring of 1862, the duties of the Quartermaster Department I was in were divided, and I was transferred to Major John C. Maynard, who was put in charge of the forage. His office was on Ninth and Main, over what is now Polk Miller's drugstore.

With Whitfield one evening a gentleman came in to see if there was a boat going down the river that afternoon as he wished to go down to Shirley [plantation] at Curle's Neck. He was dressed in a sort of fatigue suit with no mark of rank, and did not give his name. When he went out, all the clerks wondered who he could be. All of us was sure from his manner and appearance that he was some distinguished man. It was the universal verdict of all that he was the handsomest and courtliest man we ever saw, so we wished to know who he was, and we learned it was General R. E. Lee. At this time he did not wear a beard, only a mustache, which was only slightly iron gray. I saw him often that spring and summer, and he then wore only the mustache. I never saw him after he turned out the full beard as his pictures represent him. I would like to have a picture as he first was seen by me; no one was ever more handsome.

After the fights around Richmond, his office was in the Custom House, and I often saw him and President Davis on their horses going out to the camps. Davis rode a dark bay Arabian, and Lee a gray. Though Lee was considered such a fine horseman and was so distinguished looking, yet to my mind, the President was the best rider. He is the only man I ever saw who looked like he and his horse were one.

A Union army foraging party at Newport News is shown in this illustration by A. Woud, Esq. from the **New York Illustrated News** *of September 1861. Peninsula farms and homes were routinely stripped of stored food, animals, and furniture by the invading army.*

THE FARMS of W. C. Marrow and J. P. Mallicotte, which the Wests passed en route through Warwick County, were in that portion of the present Newport News, near Christopher Newport College. The Mallicotte house, which faced the present Shoe Lane, was dismantled in the 1950s when Mallicotte Lane was developed. Two Mallicottes, Sylvanus H. (1834-1886) and F. P., served throughout the war in the Warwick Beauregards, a company of volunteers organized on May 27, 1861. They saw service throughout the war as Company H of the 32nd Virginia Infantry Regiment, and the two were among 22 of the company who survived the war and surrendered at Appomattox on April 9, 1865. Sylvanus Mallicotte is buried in St. John's Churchyard, Hampton.

Robert R. Howison was a Richmond journalist and historian of the Civil War era.

When the Wests stayed overnight at William C. Marrow's in Warwick County they were visited by Mr. Ivy, who did not then occupy the house, and by Pompey Marrow, later commissioner of revenue of Warwick County. William Ivy, a surveyor, organized the Central Land Company to develop East End after the war and in 1870 laid out Chesapeake City, later called Phoebus. His son was Edward T. "Ned" Ivy. Ivy Avenue was named for the family.

Colonel John Bankhead Magruder (1810-1871) was in charge of Confederate defense of the Peninsula. A graduate of West Point, he had his early headquarters at Yorktown. Under his command, Confederates built three defense lines across the Peninsula between Newport News and Williamsburg to deter the Union invasion. On June 10, 1861, his troops repulsed an attack by Federal forces at Big Bethel, the first notable land battle of the war. In 1862 he was unable to hold off General George B. McClellan's forces at Yorktown. The Army of Northern Virginia then came south to the Peninsula and opposed McClellan's westward advance.

Charles King Mallory, later Colonel Mallory, CSA, had a farm on Sawyer Swamp Road, now Big Bethel Road, in what was then rural Elizabeth City County. He was later attorney for Parker West.

Steamboats travelling the James usually included a stop at the mouth of the Chickahominy River, a tributary of the James. The dock was about 15 miles from Williamsburg, near the present Chickahominy bridge on State route 5.

Major James Henry Lane (1833–1907), born at Goshen plantation in Mathews County, was major of the 1st North Carolina Volunteers in the battle of Big Bethel. He was later promoted to brigadier general and served with Generals John B. Magruder and Daniel Harvey Hill in General Joseph E. Johnston's Army of Northern Virginia in the Peninsula Campaign. After Johnston was wounded in the Battle of Seven Pines (Fair Oaks), Robert E. Lee succeeded to command of the Army of Northern Virginia.

The farmer who befriended the West family at Bottom's Bridge was Ned Bradley. He lived about twelve miles from Richmond.

James Causey, whom the Wests encountered in Richmond, was also a refugee from the Peninsula. His family owned Causey's mill, now part of Lake Maury at The Mariners' Museum, Newport News.

The Schmelz family of Hampton, whom the Wests also encountered in Richmond, was headed by Francis Anton Schmelz, who had come from Germany and become an American citizen about 1846. Before and after the Civil War he prospered as baker and grocer in Hampton. His sons, George and Henry Schmelz, became Hampton merchants in the postwar years. They established the Schmelz National Bank, which they extended before 1891 to Newport News. It was liquidated in 1931 and its Newport News building at Twenty-fifth Street and Washington Avenue taken over in 1932 by the Citizens and Marine Bank, founded by George Ben West.

CSA Gen. John B. Magruder

The George Bates family of Elizabeth City County, also refugees in Richmond, owned land adjoining Bates Creek, now Indian River Park, plus Armstrong's Point and Merrimack Shores. The site of the Bates house on Chesapeake Avenue is now occupied by the residence of Mr. and Mrs. E. F. Hewins.

General Virginius Groner, CSA, was acting assistant adjutant general of the Confederacy in 1862.

The James River basin at Richmond lay just below the fall line, close to lower Main Street. Upriver of the tidal basin, vessels entered the tidewater connector locks of the James River-Kanawha Canal, which led to Richmond's main canal basin. From there, boats went upriver to Lynchburg and Buchanan.

George Ben West's "Aunt Eliza," Mrs. Eliza Smelts West, lived with the Parker Wests in Richmond before going to Norfolk to be with George S. West, her son, who had been discharged from the Confederate army on account of health. She later married John Tabb and, on his death, Samuel Lively.

Polk Miller, whose drugstore at Ninth and Main streets, Richmond, was in the Confederacy's Quartermaster building, wrote and lectured on Southern life. He created Sergeant's dog remedies, named for Miller's favorite setter dog.

Robert E. Lee occasionally visited Shirley plantation, home of his cousin Hill Carter. Lee's mother, Anne Hill Carter, had been reared at Shirley.

CHAPTER VII

The War in All Its Horrors

THIS SPRING AND SUMMER (1862) WE BEGAN TO realize war in all its horrors. The evacuation of the Peninsula, the fight at Williamsburg, and fights around Richmond were participated in by our friends and acquaintances, and daily we were hearing of the death or wounding of some of these. How anxious we were to hear and yet dreaded to hear who the killed and wounded were! This was the most disastrous year to the troops from the Peninsula of any during the war.

When Magruder fell back from Yorktown and the Army of Northern Virginia had to come from the Rapidan to defend Richmond, there was great excitement and grave fear that the city would fall into the hands of the enemy. There was a rumor that General Joseph E. Johnston advised the evacuation of the city to draw the Yankees farther away from the base of supplies. At any rate, the government made provisions to move in case it became a necessity. Brother even had his ticket to Columbia, S.C., to superintend the removal of the records of the Adjutant General's office to that place. Our department was to be removed to Lynchburg.

After a full discussion of the subject by all the family, it was decided that we should move the family to Lynchburg at once. Mr. Parrish decided that he would remain, and if the city should be evacuated he and his family would return home, but decided to send Matt with our family. The family went on the passenger boat on the James River and Kanawha Canal with a few trunks of clothes; the furniture was put on a freight boat. They left on Friday evening and arrived Sunday. Brother went up by train Sunday and rented a small house. One of the greatest rainfalls ever experienced around Richmond took place that evening and night, the time of the Battle of Seven Pines.

The Yankees had crossed the Chickahominy Swamp, and there was great excitement in Richmond as well as along the lines of the three lines of entrenchment that protected the city. The inner line had not been mounted with any artillery, and I had to send out lumber to the batteries to temporarily mount some heavy guns. I was out in the rain and could not assist the family in moving, or even go down to the canal to see them off though it (the canal basin) was only a few squares off.

Before the freight boat reached it but after the passenger boat passed it, the canal was broken by the freshet above Richmond, so that it was two or three weeks before the family got their bedding and furniture. The neighbors were very kind and loaned a cot for father to sleep on, a few chairs, and some bedclothes, yet they had to rough it and sleep on the floors. A Mrs. Shafter who lived near had a good library and loaned her books to them, so they employed themselves in reading as there was little housekeeping to do. There were several families from the Peninsula living there, so on the whole they had not such a bad time. Sue had a long spell of typhoid fever that summer. Brother and I boarded with Mr. Parrish [in Richmond], and as our army whipped the Yankees in all the fights around Richmond, we very soon knew that the city was safe.

But oh, what a sad time it was! The whole city was filled with the sick and wounded, every available place a hospital, and a great many private houses with some loved one or acquaintance. The hearses were busy all the day and did not take only one body but as many as could be put in. The dead could not be buried as fast as they were hauled out and had to lie in the cemeteries sometimes 24 hours before the graves could be dug.

I saw a man brought back from Oakwood Cemetery sitting up in his coffin, who had been carried out as dead but had come to while lying out on the ground. No doubt some were buried alive, and many died for want of proper attention and care.

The people of Richmond did everything in their power to help, especially the ladies, who nursed in the hospitals and furnished all the delicacies they could get. On my way to the office I passed the Seabrook Tobacco warehouse that was used for a hospital, and through the windows I could see the hundreds laying on the cots where the tobacco hogsheads had been accustomed to be stored—nothing but

One artist's depiction of the bloody Battle of Malvern Hill, July 1, 1862, southeast of Richmond. In that battle, the Confederate army lost 5,300 men without gaining an inch of ground.

a series of sheds enclosed by a brick wall. These sad scenes were so common that we became callous to them, yet the hearts of the whole South were bleeding for her dead, wounded, and sick. May she never have such another experience.

A rather strange thing happened at the battle of Malvern Hill. In crossing a field over which the Yankees had retreated, Mr. Marrow picked up a book and put it in his haversack. It turned out to be a German reader of mine that had been stolen from our house at Newport News. (I have lost the book.) Sometime in the early spring I was taken with what the doctors then said was the chronic diarrhea, and I did not get rid of it until two or three years after the war, though I was treated by some of the most celebrated surgeons in Richmond. I was able to go to the office but was sick all the time. The surgeons had to get their orders for forage from me every month, so I knew all of them, and when I found one's treatment did not do me any good, I would ask another for a prescription. I was so bad off in August that I was given a few weeks' furlough after the [Federal] army left around

Richmond and spent it in Lynchburg with the family.

I remember the morning I was to start that when I came down to breakfast that I felt so badly that I said to Mrs. Parrish that I could not possibly walk to the depot and would have to give up the trip. She was one of the best women I ever knew. She insisted that if I could take a drink of whiskey I would be able to take the trip. I had never to my knowledge taken a drink of liquor of any kind and was very much opposed to taking it now even as a medicine. But her persuasion and my great desire to see the home folks after a long time, overcame my scruples and I took the drink and started and was surprised to find that I felt better the farther I went. I really felt better that whole day than I had for sometime. After this I always felt better when I could get a bottle of French brandy from the Medical Purveyor's Department, which I occasionally did, than from any of the medicines any of the surgeons gave me.

Father [in Lynchburg] was able to walk about the city, having lost some of his fat, and he used to loaf around Mr. Miller's grocery and sometimes bought some produce or fruit and shipped it to Richmond and so made a little money.

At the battle of Sharpsburg, all the Peninsula soldiers were engaged. Their losses were very heavy, so there was sorrow in many homes of the refugees. I returned from Lynchburg with Henry Causey on the canal boat. We had to spend one night on it, and it was a novel experience to me. There was a great deal of travel at this time, and the boat was crowded. I could not understand how we would sleep till they swung, in the center of the boat, berths in three tiers. I fortunately got in one of the side ones, for to me it looked very dangerous, seeing the men swing one above the other. I never saw such familiarity among strangers; everybody tried to have a good time and make others enjoy themselves. Many had snacks with them, or fruit, and it would always be handed to all the passengers. So, though very slow and tedious travel, there was so much of sociability and informality it was delightful. Money at this time was worth $2 for $1 in gold.

The family were to return [to Richmond] about the middle of October. About the first of the month, brother became unwell and after a few days remained at home hoping to get better. On the Friday before the family returned on Sunday, he felt better and went to his office. That evening, returning from our business, both of us had chills. The next day both of us were ill. The doctor said brother's was typhoid and mine intermittent fever, but unless mine was broken at once it would go into typhoid, as there was an epidemic of it in the city. He failed to break my fever, and though perhaps I was not at any time dangerously ill, yet I did not get down to my office until the tenth of January and was then so weak as to have to be sent home in an ambulance.

Brother grew rapidly worse and died on the Wednesday following the return of the family. His death did not seem to affect me, for I suppose I had seen and heard so much of death that it had lost its terrors, and I was so sick that for once in my life I do not think I would have cared whether I lived or died. My salary was sent to me each month, and so we made out to have something to live on.

Before Christmas there was an epidemic of smallpox in the city, and Mrs. Parrish in going about the city contracted the disease. We were all in her room that evening and the next day, until the doctor was called in. Dr. Hope thought it smallpox, but as he had never seen a case and as Mr. Parrish, who had had it in his young days, declared it was not, he waited until the next day when he vaccinated all whites and blacks except Mrs. Williams (Mrs. Parrish's mother), who, he told it, was no use as she was too old to take it. Mrs. Parrish and her mother both died of it, and everyone of their family, both white and black, had the varioloid. Strange to say, not a member of our family, though we were thrown with them daily, got it.

Soon after the Parrishes moved to Manchester [now south Richmond], where Mrs. Parrish died, and then the rest returned home or rather to Mr. John Williams', Matt's uncle.

A navy yard was started down at Rocketts [at Richmond's east end, below the James River falls], and father secured a place as watchman at the gate in the daytime and thus helped to support the family. How we got along in 1863 and '64, I hardly know. It must have been terrible on mother, father, and Mammy Watson; the younger ones could stand it better. Mr. Malone, who traded down the country, helped us a great deal by letting us have things at what they cost, and Mr. Causey also did the same. He was employed by the Provost Department and frequently went down into King and Queen [County] and adjacent counties. We had to give up all kinds of luxuries, or rather what we now think of as necessities.

The summer of '63 we had the last sugar, and this cost us, I think,

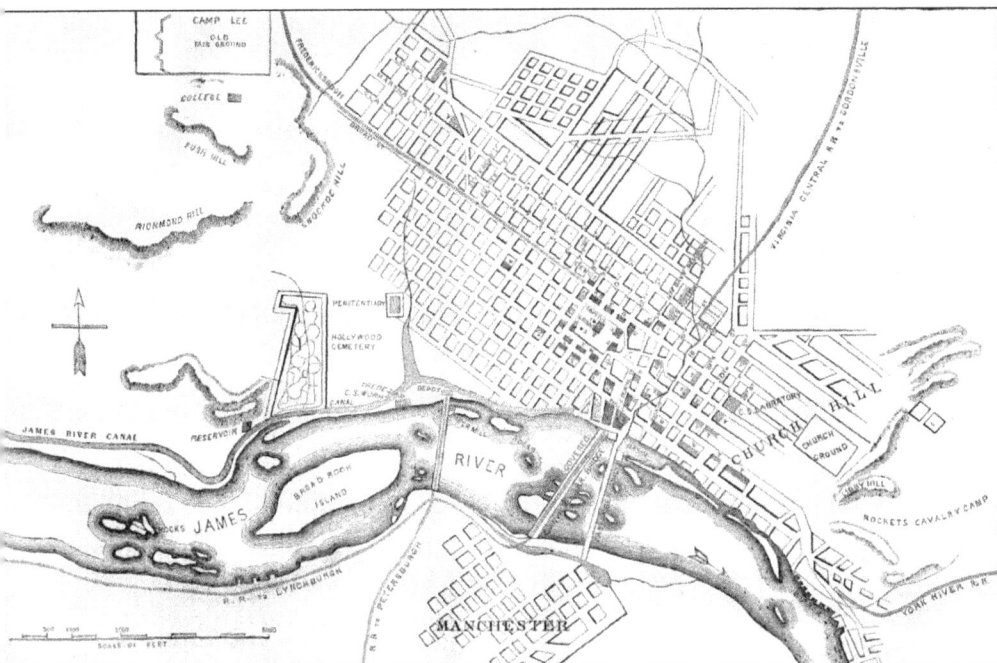

When the West family lived in Richmond, they were among a significant population of other refugees from the Hampton Roads area. This map of Richmond appeared in Harper's Weekly, *August 9, 1862.*

$20 a pound. Coffee and tea had been given up long before. Everything that would color water was used as a substitute: parched corn, peanuts, meal bran, sweet potatoes, and I know not how many other things. Father preferred the meal bran and became quite fond of it, so that at first when we got coffee after the war, for some time he would use the bran. The most of us only took water to wash down our bread, for almost all of the grease was used in making up the cornbread. Our garden furnished us some vegetables.

Our Peninsula 32nd Virginia soldiers were around Petersburg on guard duty and we saw them occasionally, and they were not in any of the fights, not even Gettysburg, so we were not so anxious. Only the cavalry, the Old Dominion Dragoons, were exposed.

By my position I was able to help them a good deal when from any cause any one of them happened to be in or around the city. In the handling of such immense stores of forage, the actual amount on hand exceeded, by immense quantities, what was reported to the Quartermaster General. I was allowed to order from this overage to my friends and acquaintances what I pleased. Of course they were entitled to it for their horses, but as there would not be an officer with them to sign the requisition, they could not have gotten it unless it had been and would be taken out of the overage. It was a source of great gratification to me to be able thus to help the boys, and they always came for it when in town. Their horses would have suffered had it not been for this, for they had no means to buy with.

Major Maynard was a most excellent man and kind to everyone, and he not only stretched his authority very often but allowed us to do the same. I do not mean that he did wrong or allowed us to do so, but in a position of this kind, and in wartimes, a great injustice could be often done to parties by being too strict in following regulations. He was very intimate with the high officials and could have been granted any request he made of them. The later part of the war he got permission from the department to rent a farm and work it for the benefit of the clerks, in order that they could live better. The war ended before we got any benefit from the farm, and the farmer got stock, crops, etc., as he was in possession at evacuation. But he (the Major) and others were the means of all the clerks' having been allowed to buy about 30 pounds of beef a month, and a bushel of meal at actual cost to the government, and this was of great help to us and no doubt saved much suffering.

Money depreciated so rapidly that our salaries amounted to hardly anything. I was told to draw money I actually needed, as there was introduced into [the Confederate] Congress a bill to pay us a much larger salary, and as this bill never passed, at the end of the war I was among a few who probably owed the Confederacy instead of its owing me. In 1861 also rented a few acres in the western part of the city and employed a negro belonging to Arthur West. I could get a horse always from the stables to do the farm work. I spent some money on it, but the ending of the war stopped also my farming, and when I got back after evacuation, the place had been neglected as the negro I hired was free, and I lost all.

There became a necessity to have a division for local defense on account of the frequent raids around the city, and General George Washington Custis Lee was the commander. All the clerks in the departments, and old men who were exempt on account of age, and boys below age, were formed into companies and regiments. I did not join for some time because Major Maynard wished me to remain in the office, and though, during the raids, even men on furlough were picked up and put in some company and sent to the front, yet he always went to the Secretary of War and got my exemption for this particular day if the Secretary had not left his office. If late in the evening, I would send up to the stables (kept by us for officers around the city who had no stables to keep their horses), and have a horse sent down and would ride it home and in this way avoid being stopped by the guards, as they would think I was a courier or something else.

Sometime in '63 or '64 there was a rumor that the government warehouses would be burned by spies in the city, so the local defense were called out to guard them at night. I thought this was a duty I could perform, so joined, or was enrolled in, one of the companies to do this guard duty. I served on guard two nights one week, and was ordered out the third night. This was more than I could stand and do my work at the office in the daytime (for I also had the diarrhea all this time), so I informed the Major and told him he must relieve me from one or the other. He wrote a letter asking for my discharge from the local defense, and I took it to all the officers, who endorsed the recommendation that morning, and he then went to the Secretary of War and got my discharge from all military duty, and I never performed any more. I went to Broad Street that evening, where we had to meet with our guns for duty, and when my name was called I handed in my discharge and my accoutrements, and had no more soldiering to do. I had never had a gun etc. till this week.

Mrs. Malone died about this time, leaving a young baby which sister Mary took, but it soon died. Mother died on February 14, 1865, after quite a long sickness. Though these were stirring and very exciting times, yet we hoped and believed we would succeed.

We did not at all realize the conditions of affairs. On April 2, '65, Sunday morning, about 12 noon, while we were sitting in the office, we heard quite a stir on the street and found out it was parties from the St. Paul's Church, in earnest conversation and deep excitement, and by inquiry found out the message sent [from Petersburg] by General Lee to President Davis about evacuating the city [Richmond]. As soon as possible, I went home and informed the family, and we talked over

Richmond scenes illustrated **Harper's Weekly,** *May 31, 1862.*

what was best to do. We had never considered such a condition of affairs, and had never talked about what should be done if the city should fall. There was no way that the family could leave the city. I had made up my mind to follow the army, so we talked over what the family should do when the city was taken by the Yankees, and as they could make nothing in the city, we decided they had better return home to the Peninsula as soon as possible.

We then thought of getting what we could to support them as long as possible. Major Maynard told me to take what meal, etc., I wanted, so we had a load carried home. I left the house about 9 p.m. with only a change of underclothes, and took all the Confederate money in the house (and was very much surprised to find that nearly everyone had some little money put away). Tom Allen, a member of the Old Dominion Dragoons, had a year before lost his horse someway and had been paid by the government, I think about $2,500 for him, and had been able to get a horse without using his money. Not wishing to carry the money about him, he had given it to me to keep. In going up to the office he passed a broker's with some gold in the window and he went in and bought a $20 piece. I think he paid $500 for it. He was killed a few weeks later.

His brother, John, I did not see during the war, and as his father, mother, and sisters were on the Peninsula, I still had the money in my possession. I took all his Confederate money with me, as well as that of the home folks, thinking if I used it I could replace the equivalent and give to his family, or might run across his brother and give it to him. Of course, the parting with the loved ones was exceedingly sad, though not a one tried to persuade me to remain. I did not know what I would do or where I would go, but I intended to follow the army and stay as long as there was any chance of success. I had no idea the cause was in such a critical state. Though I had been so situated that it would have been almost criminal to have left the family and gone into active service; and though I believed I was doing more good and greater work and was of more service than I could do in the field; and though others also thought so, as evidenced by my discharge from even field duty in the local defence; and though on account of my health I did not believe that I could stand the fatigue and hardship of camp life, yet I had not been very well satisfied with myself when I remembered that my friends and acquaintances were bearing the burdens and risks of a soldier, and I in a bombproof [shelter] in Richmond.

A Union officer rides across a wartime bridge in the Chickahominy swamp, erected by the Army Corps of Engineers. The swamp, which lies east of Richmond, was problematic for the Union army during the Civil War. Reproduced from **Harper's Weekly.**

IN JUNE and July, 1862, the Peninsula campaign approached Richmond, and the city was engulfed in injured and dying soldiers. General George B. "Little Mac" McClellan, commanding the 80,000-man Army of the Potomac, had moved up the Peninsula from Yorktown in an effort to capture Richmond and disable the Confederacy. After Confederate General Joseph E. Johnston was injured, Robert E. Lee was given command of the defending armies. While Richmond tightened its defenses, Lee fought off McClellan in the Seven Days' Battles, June 26–July 2, 1862. After his final repulse on July 1 at Malvern Hill in Henrico County, McClellan withdrew and encamped along the James in Charles City County.

As Federal forces approached Richmond in early June, 1862, many civilians fled the city. The Wests went via the James River-Kanawha Canal to Lynchburg.

Oakwood Cemetery, on Nine Mile Road east of Richmond, was the burial site of 18,000 Confederates killed in the Seven Days' Battles.

West's brother, William Drummond West, died October 10, 1862, aged 28 and unmarried. He was a clerk in the Confederate Adjutant-General's office. He was buried in Oakwood Cemetery in Richmond.

Varioloid is a mild form of smallpox suffered by a person who has been vaccinated or who has had a previous attack.

George West was a cousin of George Ben West.

George Washington Custis Lee, at that time a colonel and aide to President Jefferson Davis, was in command of the defense of Richmond in 1862. The son of General Robert E. Lee, he was made brigadier general in 1863 and major general in 1864. After his father's death in 1870, Custis Lee succeeded him as president of Washington College, which became Washington and Lee University.

A bombproof was a shelter designed to withstand artillery bombardment.

CSA Col. G. W. Custis Lee

CHAPTER VIII

Richmond's Evacuation

I THOUGHT THE FAMILY COULD NOW RETURN home [to Newport News] and live without my help, for we did not know that father's property had been confiscated and some of it sold, but thought they might at least sell some of the property to live on. So I made up my mind to go into active [military] service and to stay in it as long as possible. I have always been surprised that the family, knowing all the facts, had not tried to dissuade me from leaving them in the helpless condition they were in. How unfitted I was for hardships I would have to bear! It seemed to me that the catastrophe of the evacuation fell with such a sudden and stunning power that everyone forgot self in the thought of the great calamity of giving up the city, and the fear of the destruction of the Confederacy.

Mr. [Festus] Malone went with me to the office, and all along the streets we could see men hurrying and families watching and bidding farewell to loved ones, but everything was solemn and subdued—no noise of wailing and crying, only silent tears and deep sobs. The city seemed to be as friends beside a dying loved one, trying not to show but to suppress the anguish they felt. There was a deep hush over everything and everyone. This hush and depression was even around the offices, for though the clerks were packing such papers as they wished to carry, or were carrying them out to the Capitol Square to be burned (such as could not be carried away), still all was done in as subdued and quiet a manner as possible, and there was no noise or confusion.

After we had packed up or burned what was in the office, we waited for our wagon train to come to take us. Someone came in with a new overcoat he had gotten at Major Weisiger's on Fourteenth Street, and I and a young telegraph operator, having no overcoats, went down to get one. All had been given away, but we were offered any quantity of cloth to make what we might wish. Had Mr. Malone carried his mule and cart down with me and gone with me to Weisiger's, I believe they would have given me enough goods to fill the cart; at least we could have gotten some. We were told we might get coats at Major [J. B.] Ferguson's [a Confederate purchasing agent] on Cary Street.

It was now about 11 o'clock. The Medical Purveyor's was on Fourteenth Street, and they were now rolling out all the liquors and emptying them in the gutters; also all the liquors in all the warehouses around there. I saw men lying on the streets and drinking liquor from the gutters. I probably never was as near drunk, for the whole atmosphere on these streets was filled with the odor. I have no idea how much was destroyed by the Medical Department, but it seemed to me that they had better been more liberal in supplying the sick and not had so much to destroy. The same thing could be said of the Commissary and the Quartermaster Departments, for that night immense stores were destroyed in both departments. It also shows how unexpected was the evacuation of the city. There was quite a crowd around Major Ferguson's when we arrived. I suppose they were there for the plunder, but they were not allowed to enter.

When we got to the door and informed those inside who we were, they at once let us in and told us to help ourselves to anything we saw. There was no one in but clerks. We had been let in by an Irishman, who had been getting orders for meal from me for his family. It was a large building and seemed to be packed with everything that a soldier would need. There were a few Yankee overcoats that had been captured in the Dahlgren raid, and we each got one of these, and also blankets and shoes. In fact, the Irishman wanted us to take more than we could carry, but we loaded ourselves very well with what we wanted or thought the others we left in the office might wish. There were a great many bales of blankets that had never been opened, and he cut open one and we took what we wished. I did not open mine till Tuesday, when I found that it was rotten at the folds and was of no use.

On our return we saw many drunken, and some lying in the gutters with the liquor flowing around them. We passed Major Ferguson's in the wagons just before midnight, and the warehouse had been opened or broken in, and the people were carrying away their plunder. Had not the stores been robbed, they would have been burned in a few hours, and it

An 1862 scene of Richmond, looking northwest, from **Harper's Weekly.**

is unfortunate that the government had not given to all who remained in the city the stores that they (the army) could not carry away, as it would have helped a good many who really needed them, instead of having them destroyed or burned.

Our wagon train got mixed up with the artillery and army wagon trains, and our progress was very slow; we could have only gone a few miles when the day broke. We got away from the army trains and travelled all day, but I do not remember anything of the country—it was all new to me. I did not know where we were going, did not inquire, nor did I care. My thoughts were on those I left behind, not knowing how they would be treated and fearing the worst. All our drivers were negroes, and as we were not very far from Richmond, at night the white men were put on guard to keep the negroes from running off and carrying the mules with them. We managed to save all the teams but not all the drivers. We were able to get a little sleep Tuesday night. We had been travelling all day on what seemed roads that were little used, and with very few residents on them.

I left Richmond on a baggage wagon from our stables, but I was given a horse to ride Tuesday, and though he was quite poor yet was full of spirit. It proved to be one captured from the Dahlgren [raiding] party, and everything they had had been selected and was of the very best quality. Wednesday we got mixed up again with the army trains and had to, for reasons I know not, travel all night. We crossed that night a small stream, and in it the wagons were frequently stalled and had to be pulled out, so our progress was very slow. The road going to the stream was very narrow and with high embankments on either side. I was so tired and sleepy that I could not keep awake when we stopped, though I knew if I should fall from my horse I should certainly be run over by the wagons and killed or maimed. But I would waken up in time to catch myself as I reeled and was about to fall.

It was a dark, rainy, miserable night, and I was in danger of being seriously hurt most of the night, but I got right much sleep on the horse. Friday night we were again mixed up, this time with Longstreet's train, and had to cross a considerable stream which was bridged. On our side it was low bottom land, and across [from it was] a very high bluff, the road up which ran parallel with the stream, with the hill on one side and no protection on the river side save trees and bushes. Our [wagon] train, the last, did not arrive on top of the bluff till after daylight on account of the bad roads through the lowlands. There were a few houses in sight—I rather think it might have been called a village—but I have now forgotten the name of it and also of the stream.

We at once went into camp and prepared for breakfast. I do not think we were there an hour before it was reported that we were attacked by cavalry, and I heard a few shots. In a short time the whole camp was panic-stricken. I saddled my horse and with the rest rushed down the hill. By this time the road was almost blocked with men on foot and on horses. The teamsters did not attempt to hitch up but mounted their mules or horses, and all of us rushed pellmell for the other side of the river. Some took short cuts down the hill and swam across the stream; the road and bridge were jammed. It was the only time I ever saw a stampede, and had I not been in it, I could not have imagined the mad rush, unreasonable fear, selfish desire for their own safety, and indifference and carelessness of others that seemed to possess everyone.

I got on the river side of the road and my horse, being lean and weak, I was soon pushed off the road and, as the bluff was very steep, was in imminent risk of myself and my horse rolling down the hill into the stream. I had on no spurs and no switch, but I rammed my heels into his side, and he showed his blood and spirit and gained a footing again in the road.

When I got to the foot of the bridge it was so crowded and swaying that I thought it would certainly fall in. I recognized a South Carolina quartermaster, and he and I put our horses' heads together and tried to keep back the crowd. As he was in uniform, we did keep them back long enough to clear quite a space on the bridge, and then we crossed. We rode up to a large, fine house on an elevation perhaps three-fourths mile from the bridge. General J. C. Breckenridge and other officers, who no doubt had quartered at this house, met the crowd and called for volunteers who were armed to return and drive back the Yankees.

In all of our trip we had fallen in with many soldiers who in one way or another had been separated from their commands and would follow along with us, sometimes at considerable distance. Some of these went back, and in a short time word was sent us that the Yankees had been driven off. I was among the first to go over and was utterly surprised to find that the wagons had been pillaged and everything in the utmost confusion. I cannot imagine who could have done it if not the villagers. I picked up a white blanket with the longest wool I ever saw. It must have belonged to some officer. It was not soiled, so I put it on my saddle and no one ever claimed it.

I do not wish to see or be in another stampede, and still I am glad to have had my experience in this one. My impressions after 36 years are not to be entirely relied on, and yet it seems to me that I now know how I felt that morning. I had a great horror of being imprisoned and certainly wished to get to a place of safety, and yet I do not think I was scared as badly as most of the people seemed, and I certainly had my wits about me and could think and reason, which did not seem to me to be the case with the majority.

Sunday we crossed a ferry where the Engineer Corps of General Lee's army were then preparing to place pontoons for his army to cross. Monday, I think it was, we arrived in Danville in the evening, and found the whole city in great excitement on account of a report that [Major General George] Stoneman's cavalry were around or near town. Here we also heard the rumor of General Lee's surrender. I do not suppose that anyone believed it. We had, when we left Richmond, intended to go to Lynchburg, where we then expected to make our headquarters; but about Friday, I think, we must have gotten orders to go to Danville, where we expected to stop. But our [wagon] train went at once to the depot and loaded up with forage and passed out of the city for Greensboro, N. C.

We had no interruption in our trip, and I remember that it was the most beautiful part of the country I had ever seen. The houses were fine and large; the outbuildings and fences all in good order; the farms neatly and well cultivated; the roads wide, shaded, and good. When we left Richmond all our teams were in fine order, but the hasty marches and often lack of long forage had broken a good many down, and sometimes they would not even follow behind the wagons, so we left several along the roads with the farmers to rest up and recuperate.

The rumor of General Lee's surrender was confirmed when we arrived at Greensboro. We camped in or at least very near the town, I think in the yard of a school. The wildest sort of rumors were circulated. Mr. [Jefferson] Davis and his government were here and were uncertain what to do. After hearing from General Joseph E. Johnston and learning he would have to surrender, it was decided that the government should be transferred across the Mississippi. This was perhaps on Friday.

Major Maynard had not only the furnishing of forage for the city of Richmond and the army around and in the field but had charge of hauling of all government goods in the city. Therefore he had a great many mules, horses, and wagons under him, and had established at his stables on Navy Hill (in Richmond's east end) quite large repair shops to make and repair his wagons. He had built there six or eight nice, strong covered wagons which he called ambulances, but which were used by the departments to take their families or officers in or around the city. He had also established quite a large shoe shop where the Yankee prisoners who wished could make shoes, and a good many were employed, so that with clerks, wagonmasters, mechanics, guards, etc., he had a large number of men under him.

As soon as it was decided to cross the Mississippi, he informed us and selected four mules for each ambulance, as President Davis intended to travel in this way. He advised me to return to Richmond, but I was anxious to go, and he said he would take me but could not furnish the money, as Confederate money would be of no value on the trip. I did not like the idea of coming so far and then returning; I did not know the true condition of the Confederate government, and it looked to me as deserting the cause. But I had only Confederate money, and could not support myself. For a day or two I was much distressed and perplexed and undecided. I fortunately met on the street in Greensboro, Major John Withers, Assistant Adjutant General of the Confederacy, and as Brother had been in his office and he knew the condition of our family, I told him what Maynard had said and told him how I felt about it. He said I had better return; there was no hope this side of the Mississippi River; that the war might be prolonged for years; and that I would be of no great service in the warfare they would now be engaged in, as I could not stand such service.

I told him it looked like deserting when I was most needed. He said if I felt this way, knowing my physical condition and the condition of my family, that he would give me a discharge. He then wrote my discharge and gave it to me. I expect this was the last discharge ever given by the Confederate government. I am sure no record of it was ever made on any government book, yet to me it was very valuable and if I had it now, money could not buy it. Unfortunately, I think it was stolen some years after the war by a negro girl living with us. I had it with some rare coins I had been collecting, which were taken by her.

Maynard gave us the horses we were riding and told us to take any of the teams he had not selected and wagons, etc. Our party consisted often mounted men, and we took four mules and a wagon, and put in some forage (mostly meal) for the teams, and flour and bacon for ourselves. The team had been rested; still we put on quite a small load. One of the men whose home was in Georgia wanted my blanket, so I swapped with him for a U. S. Army blanket. Another sold me an old silver watch worth about $10 for, I think, $1,000 in Confederate money. This watch and the $20 gold piece I gave to Tom Allen's family when I got to Elizabeth City County, on the Peninsula.

We started, I think, on Monday, April 17. Our idea was to avoid all towns and keep clear of the Yankees as long as possible, for we expected to lose our horses when we came across the Yankees and wished to get as near to Richmond as possible before doing so, as we wished to walk as little as necessary. We crossed the Dan River west of Danville. We had meal that we could feed horses on, but had to get long forage either by exchanging meal or flour for it, or for Confederate money. I was surprised to find that this money would sometimes be taken.

We stopped one night in Pittsylvania at a Mr. Fitzgerald's, who seemed not to have been hurt by the war. He lived in a good-sized house, on a large farm; his barns and granaries were full; and everything showed prosperity. Though they were milking and had a quantity of milk which must have been fed to the pigs, he would not sell us a pint without we could pay for it in silver, nor would he exchange his hay or anything we wanted for flour or meat. He would not even give or sell us wood to cook our suppers and abused us greatly for cutting down a tree to do our cooking with.

A few of the boys that night turned their horses into his clover patch, and I am sorry we all did not do so. I mention this case because it was exceptional, for everyone else treated us well and though we needed long forage most for the horses really suffered for the want of it, yet it seemed the scarcest thing the people had. It was a season of the year when it is always scarce on the farm, and the soldiers returning home had no doubt used what could be gotten.

We returned by the most out-of-the-way and unfrequented roads. We went close to Appomattox Courthouse and then through Buckingham to the river, and crossed into Fluvanna. In passing over a ferry in Pittsylvania or Appomattox, we had to wait for the negro ferryman who brought over a number of soldiers returning to their Southern homes. He charged $5 in Confederate money for each, and he had literally a hat jammed full of bills. A good many of the soldiers had no money, and would walk off leaving the old man quarrelling. I have often wished to have seen the old man when he found out that all the money he was now so anxious to get was of no value.

We crossed the James above Columbia [in Fluvanna County] and went through the village below which there had been killed a hundred or two of horses. If I knew then, I have forgotten why. The stench of the decaying carcasses was truly horrible, and I do not see why it did not (and it may have) cause a good deal of sickness. At night we stopped at a farmhouse owned by a Mr. Burgess and as it was raining, we asked to be allowed to occupy one of the outhouses to sleep in. He insisted that we should take supper with him, and he seemed to have several young lady visitors who waited on us at table. This was the first meal I had eaten in a house since I left Richmond, and I thought the best I ever ate, and it was a real good country meal.

He also arranged for us to sleep in his house, and when I was shown to our room, in which there was nice beds and clean sheets, I told the boys I could not occupy one of them as they insisted, for I never felt so dirty in all of my life. I had not changed my clothes for weeks and had to wash them the last time in a stream or pond and had not gotten out very much dirt. I wrapped myself in my dirty blanket and lay before the fire and slept well, for this was a great deal better than under a wagon or a bush tent. I somewhat realized how a sinner with all his vileness and filth would feel in the presence of a holy being. Had the bed been somewhat dirty and with no sheets, in an outhouse, I think I would have enjoyed sleeping on it, but it was too clean and I realized how dirty I was.

I shall never forget the kindness of Mr. Burgess and would have been, and still would be, glad to do something to show my appreciation for it. I have never seen or heard of him since. One of the young men with us lived near Ashland and was taken sick, so we concluded to take him home, though it was out of our way. Yet it would take us through a section that would be less apt to have Yankees foraging about the country. We struck across Goochland [County] and may have gone into the lower end of Louisa [County] into Hanover [County].

We had a man with us who lived in Chesterfield [County] who was riding a very large fine white mule that showed no sign that he had ever been branded, but his shoulders were badly galled, having been used in a wagon train. The horse I was riding was, I think, a blooded one. He had been given me the first day out of Richmond and he had been captured from the Dahlgren raiders and had "U.S." stamped very plainly on his shoulder. We exchanged my horse for his mule, as he wished it. He thought he lived in such an out-of-way place that the Yankees would not find him, and as I did not expect to keep either horse or mule when we should meet the Yankees, it made very little difference to me what I should ride till then.

The ruins of Richmond, printed in **Harper's Weekly,** *April 22, 1865.*

THE KILPATRICK-Dahlgren raid was led by Brigadier General Hugh Judson Kilpatrick, whose second-in-command was Colonel Ulric Dahlgren. The raiders set out from Culpeper County on February 28, 1864. Kilpatrick sent Dahlgren with 500 men to raid Goochland County, keeping the main force with himself. The two forces were to reunite before Richmond. However, they were driven off separately by the Confederates. Kilpatrick escaped down the Peninsula to the Union lines at Williamsburg. Dahlgren sought to escape to the Union garrison at Gloucester Point but was killed by Confederates in King and Queen County. He was buried in Richmond, but the body was removed from the grave by Union sympathizers, who kept it concealed until after the war, when it was taken north for reburial.

George Ben West in his flight from Richmond through southside Virginia encountered the train, or supply wagons, of General James Longstreet, CSA. Longstreet had served under Lee in the 1864-65 defense of Richmond and Petersburg and had surrendered with Lee at Appomattox.

General John Cabell Breckenridge, CSA, whom West encountered between Richmond and Danville, had been vice president of the United States from 1857–61, in the presidency of James Buchanan.

Major General George Stoneman, USA, commanded Union cavalry units which were harassing western Virginia at the time Lee surrendered at Appomattox.

General Joseph E. Johnston, CSA, was obstructing General William T. Sherman's campaign through North Carolina at the time of Lee's surrender. Johnston capitulated to Sherman April 26, 1865.

When George Ben West reached Greensboro, N.C., in April, 1865, President Jefferson Davis and members of his cabinet were already there. Like West, they had fled Richmond before Lee's surrender, gone first to Danville, and then on to Greensboro. Davis and some of his cabinet at first considered moving the Confederate command west of the Mississippi and continuing the war, but this was averted when Davis was captured May 10, 1865, in Irwinville, Georgia, and confined at Fort Monroe awaiting trial.

CHAPTER IX

Rules Had Been Abolished

I HAVE MENTIONED THE FACT THAT MAJOR Maynard had been allowed by the government to rent a farm for the purpose of raising vegetables to give or sell at a nominal cost to the clerks in the departments. This farm was several miles from Richmond on, I think, the Brook Road. We determined to stop there and find out if possible what was going on in Richmond. While a few went with the sick man to his home, we went toward Richmond to the farm, which was run by a man named Adams, I think. At the home of the sick man, Waldrop, who accompanied him, learned that they issued passes in Ashland for persons who wished to go to Richmond. So he rode up there and secured a pass for himself and his servant.

We learned from Adams that anyone could go into the city though it was guarded on all the roads. He told us that our horses and mules or wagon would not be taken away, and that anyone could be paroled under the terms of General Lee's surrender. Waldrop and I rode ahead, I to represent his servant in the pass. We, or rather most of us, saw a Yankee soldier for the first time since we left Richmond. These were Germans, and I doubt whether they could read the pass, but at any rate they told us to go in the city. We went a few hundred yards and waited to see what they would do for the rest. They were only questioned a little while, and then with wagon, they came up to us. We soon began to drop out as we reached our different homes till at last I was left alone as I lived out near Battery 4, on Church Hill.

I never knew what was done with the four mules and wagon. I suppose they were sold and proceeds divided among some of the party. All I got was the mule, which I kept till she died in 1870. How delighted I was to get home! I had not heard a word from them, or they from me,

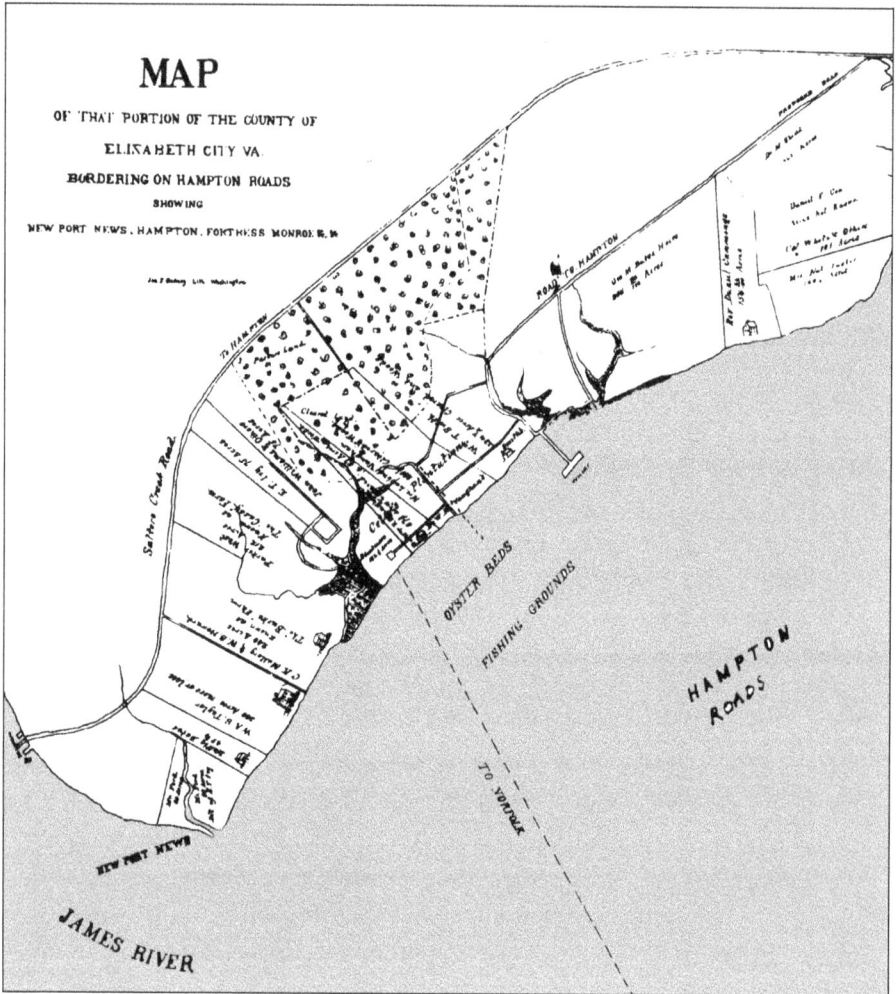

Map drawn about 1870 shows landholdings between Newport News and Hampton. The former Parker West farm occupied land near Newport News Point, then in Elizabeth City County.

since I left, and to find all well and that they had not suffered by reason of the occupation by the Yankees was happiness indeed. I must have presented anything but an agreeable appearance. While riding home after the rest had left me, my old mule would bray at every corner, and I thought I attracted the attention of everyone on the streets and in the houses. As there were guards along the principal streets, I feared to be arrested all along the way.

I returned [to Richmond] the very last day of April and I suppose was one of the last to get back to the city. Father and Mr. Marrow (who had returned soon after the surrender) were down in Elizabeth City County to see after what they had left behind at the beginning of the war. Mr. Marrow had been cut off from the army at, I think, Saylor's Creek and therefore was not at the surrender. They got back to Richmond in a few days, and father thought it best that I should go down to look after some things that he had not been able to attend to.

Our lot we lived on in Richmond contained about a quarter of a square [city block], and during the war we always raised a nice lot of vegetables. Father, in the fall of '64, set out quite a quantity of lettuce. I do not remember whether or not that winter was unusually warm, but at any rate the lettuce was fit to sell April 1, and we had on that day sent some down to market by Cindy, our negro girl (a girl about 12 or 14 years) and got for them a dollar head. A few days after evacuation, and when the excitement of this and the burning of the city had subsided, they again sent Cindy out to market to sell them, and they sold for 5¢ a head. Though young and inexperienced, she sold about $75 worth and thus enabled us to live and have a little money to buy sugar and coffee and tea, which we had been deprived of since 1862.

Our servants stayed with us several weeks. I had intended to get a parole, but father insisted that I could go about much freer and would not be subjected to so many interruptions by the guards around Old Point if I took the oath. As he knew from his experience, being just from there, I concluded to be governed by him. No one up to this time had asked me for parole or oath, though I had walked all about the city. I went up to take the oath, and General Joseph R. Anderson, CSA, of the Tredegar Iron Works, a splendid-looking man and soldier, was ahead of me, and I heard the questions asked him, and saw the manner of the (Federal) lieutenant, who felt his importance, and I became so indignant with the lieutenant and sorry for the general that when my time came I did not feel the humiliation and shame I expected.

When I got to Fortress Monroe the rules had been abolished, and I did not have to show my certificate of oath nor did I ever have to produce it, and for many years I was sorry I ever took it. It has been lost or stolen, and this is one thing I did not regret to lose. There was a great deal of competition by rival boat companies on the route from Richmond to Fortress Monroe during this year, and I made three or four trips with only the cost of $1. They generally carried passengers free.

What a change on the Peninsula! The space between Mill Creek and Hampton—instead of cultivated farms—was covered with temporary houses and tents (Camp Hamilton), used for hospitals and quarters. Hampton had been burned by General John B. Magruder, as it had become a refuge for negroes and Yankees in '61. The Peninsula troops were of the burning party, and many a young man set fire to his own father's house. This was the case with my brother; he fired our Hampton house in the parlor. Only one Hampton house had been saved. Owned and occupied by a very poor old widow, Mrs. Latimer, it was on the south back street and not very near another building. The soldiers guarded it and put it out when it caught fire. There were very few brick houses, so the whole town was leveled, with only chimneys standing as sentinels, and they too were soon pulled down to make flues for the little shanties and tents which soon began to appear on the site.

The old St. John's Church walls remained standing and also the walls of the house of Mr. Kennon Whiting. The bridge across the creek had been rebuilt, and as I walked up the street I could not locate a single place, and when I reached the cross streets [King and Queen], I could hardly believe it was so near the foot of the bridge. The old St. John's Church was the only place I recognized. What feelings I had as I went along! I don't suppose I could have expressed them even then and certainly not after the lapse of 37 years. Sad, sad, such times, yet youth is sanguine. The uncertainty of the war times was over, the blow had fallen, and we knew the worst—or thought we did—but we could not anticipate or imagine the Carpetbag rule.

I made the house of a distant cousin, Arthur West, at New Market, my home while down on the Peninsula, and they all—children and parents—were exceedingly kind. Father, I think, was the owner of about 25 houses at the breaking out of the war. All of these were now in ashes except a very small house on the Casey farm, which was occupied by the slaves of my sister, Mary, and this was I think within a year burned; and a storehouse on the beach at the foot of the [Newport News] wharf that he built in 1860 for a store and which was used as a commissary during the war. There was not a vestige of the farmhouse

This photograph by Alexander Gardner shows a Hampton freedmen's village, possibly the one built on Parker West's farmland during the West family's absence.

or any buildings, and had it not been for a few trees remaining in the yard, it would have been impossible to have decided where they had been located.

I know of no parallel in history to the case of the refugees from this section. They came back without slaves whom they had been educated to rely upon for all work; without a cent of money; their houses in most cases gone; their fields grown up in bushes; the ditches all filled; with no stock; most of them in debt, and property mortgaged; and a good deal of the property sold or in the Federal courts to be sold for taxes. What had the men of the families to hope for or expect but absolute starvation? How was it possible for them to have the energy to even attempt anything?

Look around at the sight now. No people ever recuperated in such a short time. This whole section soon became a garden spot, and though most of the people had to lose even their land for security debts (often for hire of slaves before the war), yet though not accustomed and often not really able to work, they made the best of the situation and determined if possible to start in life again and show the Yankees that they could live without their aid, and even without slaves or property.

I think the South believed that the North had opposed slavery not so much because of their [abolitionists] love for humanity as they pretended but because they were envious of the prosperity of the South and hated the aristocracy because they knew they were the superior, and felt that their own mean pecuniary dealings and money-making propensity was condemned.

The South did not try to make money because money was the means by which they could elevate themselves, because they looked more to a man's character and behavior than to his bank account. The North had to work harder and live more economically to get along, and probably on this account they would take advantages and do little mean tricks which were looked upon by us as wanting in honor and honesty, and gentlemanly instincts. The better classes of the North never visited the South, nor were the Southern people anxious to mingle with them at the North, so we grew wider and wider apart every year. They hating and envying us more and more, and we looking down upon them.

Father, though too fat to take much exercise and now almost totally blind, yet had not lost either energy or hope and was always planning something to do. The Newport News farm had been confiscated and sold for taxes and was in the possession of an agent for the purchasers. The Casey farm was in the Federal courts and liable to be sold at any time. The lot in Hampton was also sold. The Casey farm was occupied by negroes under the Freedmen's Bureau. The Newport News farm had on it a prison camp, established in 1865 and kept till July [1865]. In addition there was a pasture ground and corral for cattle, besides a rendezvous for negroes.

When I came down I did a very foolish thing and one that might have cost me my life if I had not had on a Yankee overcoat. I was informed that someone was cutting wood on the Casey farm, and I went down to try to stop it. I rode in the woods and found about 30 axemen. I was alone, not known to or knowing a single man, not armed, and with no authority except the right of representing my father. I questioned the first man I came to and found out he was cutting it for Jerry Lee, a slave of my sister's, who lived on the farm.

I made a memorandum of the axeman's name and where he lived, told him the wood was mine, and ordered him out. Then I went to the next one and so on till in a short time all left their work and came to inquire. When I began to ask their names, they became frightened and refused to give them, but everyone left the woods and did not return to cut.

Father as soon as possible began suit in U.S. Court for the Casey farm, and after many months and by paying the cost of the suit, taxes, and about $500, got possession of it. In early fall we moved the whole family to William Turnbull's. Sister Mary and Marrow and their daughter Bettie remained in Richmond, as Marrow soon got work at his trade—carpentering. Lizzie [Elizabeth Roberta West] had gotten a position as teacher in Dr. [Beverly Preston] Morris' family in Amherst County, so we only had father, Mammy Watson, Sue, and myself. Robert Allen Davis (a cousin in Elizabeth City County) allowed me to cut wood and, borrowing a cart, I hauled it to Hampton and sold it to get groceries. This was the most humiliating business I ever did—to haul wood around town and sell to negroes.

Father had applied for a pardon as it seemed it was necessary to have one in order to have his property turned over to him—that which had not been sold. Someone must have also asked for one for him; I have two pardons for him of different dates.

Father became so blind he went to Baltimore to have the cataracts cut off his eyes. A Dr. Smith cut off one, but the nerve in the lid was so weakened that he could not raise it to see, and he said it was useless to cut off the other, so father was blind for the rest of his life. Dr. Smith, knowing his financial condition, made a very low, nominal charge for his services, though he did all he could for him. So did Cousin Levin Drummond's family. All were very kind to Sue and father while with them, which was several weeks. Cousin Levin died a few days after they left, his rheumatism or gout reaching the heart.

No one could have been kinder and more helpful to us than William Turnbull's family [in Elizabeth City County], from him to the smallest child. Mrs. Turnbull had lost her mother (father's sister) when about two years old, and she and R. A. Davis, a young brother, had been taken by mother and cared for as her own till her father remarried. She never forgot this and I believe loved us better than her half-brothers and sisters. My mother was the only mother she ever knew. I shall never forget the debt I owe each one for what they did for us in our need and hope that I can, in a proper manner, show them how I have always felt towards them. As opportunity offers, may I be a help to them. Arthur West's family were also very kind and considerate of father and myself when we stopped with them. Arthur West died, I think, in the fall of 1865.

Images like this one, printed in **Harper's** **Weekly,** *were very often copied from photographs, which were too hard to reproduce at that time. This possibly was drawn from a photograph of the banks of the James River where George Ben West's farm was located.*

BROOK ROAD was a rural Henrico County thoroughfare in 1865 but is now within Richmond.

Church Hill, the eastern part of Richmond in which the Wests lived during the war, was named for Henrico Parish Church, later known as St. John's.

Brigadier General Joseph Reid Anderson, CSA, of Richmond, had established the Tredegar Iron Works on the James at Richmond before the Civil War. It was a prime source of Confederate munitions.

George Ben West's oath of loyalty to the union, misplaced at the time he wrote his memoirs, was subsequently found.

When Hampton was burned in 1861 by order of Colonel John B. Magruder, CSA, little remained standing except the brick walls of St. John's Church, built in 1728 as the parish church of Elizabeth City County. It was rebuilt after the war and is still in service.

Camp Hamilton, a large camp of Union troops, was established in May 1861 on the west bank of Mill Creek, on the Joseph Segar farm. It covered what is now the business section of Phoebus and extended westward for some distance toward Hampton.

The Casey farm, owned by Parker West, was an area of 214 acres close to Salter's Creek and Hampton Roads, in the East End of Newport News. When the Wests returned to the Peninsula in 1865 they found the farm occupied by black families, it having been taken over by the Freedmen's Bureau, which had been created by the U.S. government in March 1865 as a "bureau of refugees, freedmen, and abandoned lands" to aid freed black people.

George Ben West's niece, Bettie Bell Marrow, the daughter of his sister Mary and her husband, William Marrow, later married William B. Vest, who was secretary of the Citizens and Marine Bank which West and other stockholders founded in Newport News in 1896.

William Turnbull was a cousin of George Ben West who resided in Elizabeth City County. The two families were intimate, as indicated by the Turnbulls' opening their house to the Wests when the latter returned to the Peninsula after Appomattox. The Turnbull farm was on Pine Chapel Road, east of the present Hampton Coliseum.

CHAPTER X

Not a Thought of the Future

I FREQUENTLY CAME DOWN TO NEWPORT NEWS [from Elizabeth City County] to see how things were going on. Around where we lived [at Newport News farm] was a prison camp which had been established about the last of March, 1865, and was used till about July 4, 1865. It extended into the James River and ran back to about where Gordon's slaughterhouse is. It contained about 20 acres and was enclosed by a high board fence. I do not know how many Confederate soldiers were imprisoned in it, but the War Department sent me at my request a list, which is copied in the book of the Greenlawn Cemetery, showing over 160 who died in this short time. The mortality must have been frightful, and most of them died after Lee's surrender.

All along the shore upon the bank from the Chesapeake and Ohio No. 10 pier up to the Hawkins house there were squatted quite a number of negro shanties, occupied mostly by negroes who had run away from the counties on the opposite side of the river, and numbered about 200 or more.

Father's wharf, opposite Eighteenth Street, was standing but was getting a bit shaky. The Burk wharf, now the place covered over by Pier 4, was not fit to use. Where Pier 6 is now, the Yankees had built quite a large wharf, and between the coal dock and No. 4 they built a very large pier to use as a coal yard (on the outer end). The pier head covered about an acre, and they stored coal in it for the use of the ships. I think some of the Confederate prisoners worked on this pier. I think Washington Burk, who owned the farm, moved down from Richmond in '65 and opened a store with Warren Gill as partner in a house on his place built as a sutler's store, and just across the lane from the commissary. This same house—with some additions—was used by

Mr. T. H. Gordon as a commissary when the Chesapeake and Ohio railroad was being built.

The farmhouse on the hill above this was used by a captain with a wife and child, who was in charge of the Freedmen's Bureau in this section and by two old women who had come from New York to teach the negro children. Being down at Burke's store in January '66, I saw the door to our house open, so I went in and found nothing in it except two plain wooden tables that had been used perhaps as office tables. I went back at once and informed father, who had just returned from Baltimore. After consulting Colonel Charles K. Mallory, father's lawyer, we moved into the house, before the agent (Nick White, who had charge of the farm for the purchaser at the confiscation sale) had any idea of our intention. He took it very coolly and did not in any way try to dispossess us.

After we became fixed I thought we were very comfortable, though only one room in the house was plastered. (I may have mentioned elsewhere that this was a two-story house and the old mule stable and crib were in the lower story, as was the wood house.) There were a few scattered pines around the marsh on Newport News Creek which had not been cut because they would fall in the marsh when cut, but the rest of the timber had been cut down and used. A negro named Jordan Hall, who lived on the hill, offered to cut the wood for me and wait till I sold it before receiving his pay. In this way I was able to get a little money to live on, as I hauled the wood on the wharf and sold it to passing boats.

This was a very hard year for us as we had no certain way to make money, and everything was high and we had to buy everything. We had to do without meat very often and sometimes were reduced to a pot of black peas and bread. Father bought a cow from R. A. Davis on an old account (or rather note) he owed him, and this was a great help as the grass was plentiful and I could stake her out. I informed the negroes that father owned the place and would collect part of the crop if they cultivated any of the farm. I did not think to require rent for ground occupied by their houses and yards. There was no civil law; the Freedmen's Bureau conducted all courts and decided all questions, and there seemed to be no appeal.

To show how arbitrary they were I give this incident. By some means, the captain whose name I have forgotten, found out I had a table that had been left by the commissary department, and he told me he wished it. I told him that a very rough table was in the house when I moved in and may have belonged to the government, but I did not know nor he, and I would not give it up. Shortly after this he got a squad of soldiers and came in the house and took the table out. I had contracted the ague and fever around New Market and had chills every two or three weeks and was then abed with it. I reported by letter the fact to the President (Andrew Johnson), but suppose he as well as those he referred it to only made fun of my ignorance in supposing they cared if a soldier entered a Rebel's house and took out even his own furniture, if he wished it. This captain tried trivial cases between negroes; the cases between whites and negroes were tried by Captain Charles B. Wilder, who held court across the Hampton Bridge, in Tabb's house.

E. S. Hamlin came down the Peninsula this spring (1866) to buy land for a projected rail terminus and did buy the farm of Captain Wilbern, and agreed to buy father's Newport News farm. He put up a forfeit of $500, and with this amount father was able to get the Casey farm out of the Federal court. I knew nothing about farming and had never done a very hard day's work in my life, but I was on a farm and with a mule, and father thought I ought to try to farm. Although blind, he knew the land and told me where to work. It was very sad to see him going over the field and stooping down to feel the ground so as to tell me how I was to plough it. I do not know whether the mule had ever plowed before, but I am sure it was my first and it was a hard day's work for the both of us. When I came home that night I felt that if I had thus to live I would not care if I died at once, and the total dependence of the entire family on me only kept me from giving up at once. And often during this year, the only comfort and hope I had was the promise of God as expressed by David, "that he had not seen the righteous forsaken nor his seed begging bread," and I trusted in my parents' righteousness and God's promise.

The land selected for farming was in fine sod and ought to have been broken up by two horses, but I had only a large, strong mule. Sometimes I would be getting along very well, I thought, when the point of the plow would strike on a shell in the land and out the plow would jump, and then the mule would take out almost in a trot for the house. As soon as I could get the shell off the point, in order to stop him I would raise the handles and down the plow would go, so deep as to bring the mule to a standstill, and I would run up on the handles and strike one in my stomach and tumble over, with the breath knocked out of me. Again, sometimes the plow would strike a hidden stump in the land and run the handles into me. I was truly nearly dead when I got to the house, but after awhile I learned something about plowing and got in a crop. I was also able to hire a hand and made very good crops, as the land was rich.

I will give a few experiences with Captain Wilder. I had to go to Richmond to get a release of the Casey farm from the Freedmen's Bureau. I do not recollect whether a military governor had been appointed or I had to apply to the head of the bureau in the State. I think it was a Colonel Brown I saw. He was quite polite and gentlemanly, I thought, and readily said he would send the order to Captain Wilder to turn over the Casey farm to father. I had had very little dealings with Captain Wilder up to this time, but I had heard much of him, and from his reputation was well assured he would hold the order and keep us out of the property as long as possible. I was in a dilemma. If I returned without the order I would be kept out of the property. If I asked for the order I would have to give the reason, that Captain Wilder would not do his duty and obey the order. So I asked if the Colonel would not give me a duplicate. He said it was entirely unnecessary as the order would reach Captain Wilder before I could see him. Then I told him my reasons for asking for it—that from what I had heard of the Captain I had reason to believe he would deny having received it. I do not know whether any complaints had ever been made before to the Colonel, but at least he did not resent what I told him and ordered his clerk to give me the duplicate.

I was right in my conjecture. A few days after I got home I went to see Wilder and in a confident manner told him he had received the order restoring the Casey farm to my father. He said he would look, and pretended to, but said he had not received it. I then informed him the date and that I was in the office and had the assurance of Colonel Brown that it would certainly be sent. He pretended to look through his desk again and said he had not received it. Then I told him I had the duplicate, which would answer. He seemed very much put out and soon found the original.

The rents of the land so held were paid by the negroes to the [Freedmen's] Bureau, but of course most of it went into the pockets of the agents. That spring the negroes living on the Jack Parrish place would drive or ride their horses across the creek at night as there was nice grazing on the Newport News farm. Early in the morning they would drive them back, and thus they required very little feed for their teams. After our corn got up the horses would graze on it. Some of the negroes on our farm were cultivating small patches near mine, and as we could not get the negroes of the Parrish farm to stop turning out their teams at night, I proposed to those cultivating with me that we would watch our fields and either take up or shoot some of the teams. Jordan Hall watched the first night, but he said he saw none. The next night I went on guard and armed, for I did not know but some of the negroes crossed the creek with their teams. I had a double-barrel shot gun and I borrowed a pistol from Jordan. About an hour or two from daybreak I found six or eight horses and mules in my oat field, and not being able to drive them out readily, I shot at the horse with the pistol. After awhile I was able to drive him up to my house and put him in the stable. I did not know I had hit the horse.

I went to bed, and sometime after sunrise I was wakened and told some negroes had come for the horse. At first I sent them word they could not get him, but after they informed me he had been shot and who he belonged to, I let them take him. A few days after I was summoned to Wilder's court to answer for killing the horse. I met Colonel Mallory there, as he had some case, and he asked what I was there about, and I told him. He took a more serious view of it than I had and offered to defend me. I do not know what they would have done had I not had an attorney, but I was required to pay $80 for a horse that I could have bought for $20. I at least saved mine and the negroes' crops on our farm, for they never more were disturbed by horses.

It was the hardest matter to keep the negroes from cutting wood off the Casey farm. George Sealy, whom we had put [as tenant] on the farm, caught Joe Wilson, a negro who lived near, cutting up a tree. In order to intimidate others, I thought I would have him tried before Wilder. It was proved beyond a doubt that he stole the wood and knew it was father's, and the court decided he should give me the value of what we had proven he had stolen, amounting to a few dollars. Neither of us had a lawyer, but Joe was a much better one than I. I asked the Captain if this was all the penalty. I told him that we had had stolen a great deal of wood, and the presumption was that Joe had stolen much

This 1861 photograph shows central Hampton soon after it was burned. The view is from South King Street, looking towards the current Hampton University site.

of it, and if he had to pay only for what he was proved to have stolen, he would continue, as he would only have to pay when caught. He (the Captain) said he would inflict no other penalty, and I ought to be satisfied to get the money for the wood. I told him I would not take a cent, but I warned Joe and all others if I caught them stealing from me, that I would shoot to kill them. The Judge did not even reprimand me, and I believe this kept many from trespassing any more, for they remembered about my shooting the horse.

Old Joe was quite a lawyer, and till a few years before he died was continually in lawsuits. When the State was relieved of its military government, Joe was elected a magistrate and he rode about with a cavalry sabre and two revolvers around his waist. I was never in one of his courts, but it must have been very farcical if it had not been so humiliating. He hired a negro boy to read to him the code every night (he could not read himself), and such was his memory that he really learned a great deal about law. He became such a nuisance before the [Freedmen's] Bureau was abolished, by having so many of his own cases and being brought up by others, that even Wilder became disgusted and sometimes rendered cases against when they should have been for him.

But before this occurred I will mention a case that rather got the best of Joe. Joe had belonged to the Wood family and had a few years before the war been bought by Mr. William Causey. He usually went by the name of Joe Wood, but perhaps because his parents belonged to a family of Wilsons, or perhaps because he disliked the Wood family, during the war he changed his name to "Joe Wilson" and went by that name. Mr. William Causey purchased his farm (that had been confiscated) from the purchaser and again went to farming. One day, while shipping some truck [crops] from the Newport News wharf to New York, he was on the wharf and was asked by some farmers (Williams, Jones, and others) to mark their truck [crop] and ship it, preferably to the same party he was sending his own to. Joe also had some stuff and asked Mr. Causey to ship his.

Several weeks afterwards he (Causey) was summoned to appear before Wilder to answer the charge of stealing the trucks, or at least receiving the money for them and using it, of the stuff he had marked for Joe. He went around the neighborhood and asked the farmers who had shipped at the same time whether or not they had gotten checks for what they had sent, and found they all had. He asked them to go down with him on the day of the trial as his witnesses. He asked others, both white and black, whom he had assisted in this way, also to go down.

On the appointed day he had six or eight witnesses with him. There was no post office here [in Newport News] then, but on his

A C&O engine and tender in the style of those that first came to Newport News in 1881.

way to the court, across the Hampton Creek, he inquired if there was a letter in the post office there for Joe, and found there was one for Joe Wood, the name Mr. Causey had shipped the trucks in. The trial commenced with neither party having a lawyer. Joe proved that he had so many barrels and at his request Mr. Causey had marked them and written the letter, that he had never heard from them since, and that Mr. Causey must have received the check and used it. Mr. Causey proved he had on the same day shipped for parties and that they had all gotten checks for their stuff.

Wilder leaned to the negro and was about to decide that Mr. Causey should pay at the rate the other parties got from their stuff. Then Mr. Causey suggested that he first send a soldier to the post office and ascertain if there was not a letter for Joe, either in the name of Causey, Wood, or Wilson. Whether or not Joe knew the letter was there is not known, but as soon as the soldier was sent, he got out and intended to reach the office before the soldier. But Causey, seeing him, asked that he be recalled, which was done. The soldier brought the letter, and it was found to contain a check for the number of packages shipped. So Wilder turned the check over to Joe and was about to dismiss the case when Mr. Causey called his attention to the fact that he and his neighbors had been put to a great deal of trouble and inconvenience and loss by having to appear at court, and asked that damages should be given. Wilder was perhaps mad to think that he had been about to render so unjust a decision at first, and perhaps believing Joe knew about the letter being in the post office, so he said he thought Mr. Causey right and made Joe give up the check and endorse it and turned it over to Mr. Causey, who went in the town [Hampton] and spent it all in treats to the crowd. I do not know whether or not Joe took any, but do not think Mr. Causey offered him.

To show how old Joe understood the law, though he had to have it read to him, after the civil government began, the sheriff of Elizabeth City County was [Captain Jerome] Titlow, who had put irons on President [Jefferson] Davis in prison. Someone got a judgment against Joe for rent, and Titlow went out to levy on something for the debt. Joe had a very good-looking potato patch, so Titlow levied on it. When fit to dig, Joe had them dug and sold them. Shortly after, Titlow came out to have them dug and found Joe had sold the crop and he threatened him with arrest and prosecution. Joe said to him that you could only levy on what you saw and that he did not see the potatoes but the vines, and the vines were still on the ground and he could get them if he wanted to. Titlow consulted a lawyer and found Joe right. After this, some negroes in the neighborhood started a cooperative store in a building at the foot of the wharf, where now Chesapeake and Ohio Pier 6 is. After awhile, Joe in some way was put in charge and it began to get in debt and the stock much reduced. The sheriff of Warwick (the store being in Warwick County) came down to levy on the stock one morning. He went in and found a very small stock and was told by the clerk that Joe was in Hampton buying some goods for the store. Joe lived on the road to Hampton, about a mile and a half distant.

The sheriff said he wanted to see him and would wait his return, and he took a seat in front of the house. The clerk sent a message to Joe that the sheriff was waiting for him and he knew about what he wanted, so he unloaded his purchases at home and drove down to the store. Finding the sheriff out in front, he drove to a back window and got the clerk to bring him the most valuable of the stock and he loaded up his cart and drove off. I think he made two trips. Then, late in the evening the sheriff, thinking Joe had heard about his being there and did not intend to come down, went in and levied on what was there but missed a great many things he saw in the morning. He never found what had been taken out by Joe.

With all Joe's rascality, he managed to keep out of jail and was never convicted but once, and then he was not as much to blame as the supervisors of the county, and they had him punished to shield themselves. The line of the county had been changed and he was living in Warwick County. He was then overseer of the poor and was instructed to buy provisions for poor and sick, and he brought in a very heavy bill for luxuries. There had been no limit put on him by the board, and they really were most to blame, but he was sent to jail for a few months. During his sentence he worked on the farm for the sheriff and was only in jail at night and on court days. One day the judge went up to the courthouse unexpectedly and Joe, who was working in the field nearby, heard of it and ran to the sheriff's house and asked that he be locked in the jail. This conviction kept him out of politics as he was not allowed to vote. Though so sharp and smart, he did not have much influence over the negroes and was really never a leader.

GEORGE BEN WEST was distressed at the sight of Newport News farm when he returned from Richmond in the summer of 1865. He describes the Federal prison camp, then on the site, and the shanties which lined the James River from the prison camp to the residence of the Hawkins family, which then stood at about the present Thirty-fifth Street and James River.

The Confederate soldiers who died in the military prison at Newport News Point were later reinterred in Greenlawn Cemetery, Newport News. They numbered 163.

The captain in charge of the Freedmen's Bureau at Newport News was Charles B. Wilder, USA. He had been assistant quartermaster and superintendent of Negro affairs at Fort Monroe during the war.

This obelisk in Greenlawn Cemetery, Newport News, commemorates the 163 Confederate prisoners-of-war.

The Colonel Mallory referred to was Charles K. Mallory of Elizabeth City County, born in 1820 and a prominent attorney and politician. He was a member of the Virginia Convention of 1861 which voted for secession, was a colonel in the 115th Virginia militia early in the war, and then became a captain in the Confederate Quartermaster Department. Three of his slaves ran away from his farm to Fort Monroe in 1861 and were declared by the fort's commander, General Benjamin Butler, USA, to be contraband of war. After the Civil War, Mallory resumed his Hampton law practice until his death in 1875. Mallory Avenue in Hampton was named for him.

Tabb's house, at 427 East Queen Street in Hampton, where

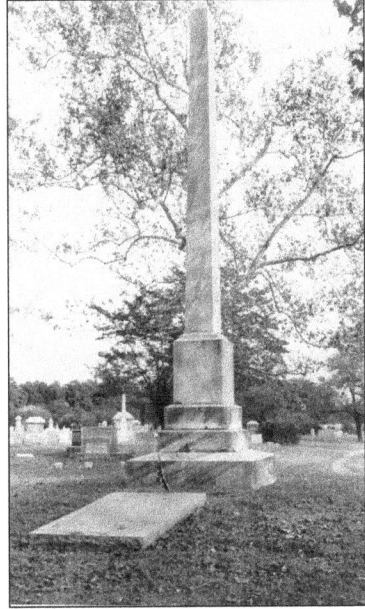

Captain Wilder held Freedmen's Bureau court, is still standing. It was earlier the residence of Colonel Thomas Tabb, attorney during the Civil War period.

Edward S. Hamlin, a Northern real estate speculator, had come to Newport News Point in the 1860s and bought options on waterfront acreage in hopes of creating a deepwater rail terminus. Under Federal statutes of confiscation, Parker West had lost his life estate in Newport News farm, but the fee passed to his heirs. But Parker West had become surety on the bonds of others who, having lost their property during the war, were unable to meet their obligations. Lawsuits were brought against the aged man, and to satisfy the judgments against him, his Newport News farm was divided into ten parcels and sold. Mr. Hamlin got an option and purchased all these tracts at $300 an acre except George Benjamin West's 15 acres, which constituted Eighteenth Street; J. B. Whitehead's 20½ acres known as "Dawson City;" and the Groome tract of five acres nearby. After the Chesapeake and Ohio Railway chose Newport News as its eastern terminus, it gradually bought up these remaining holdouts.

The assistant commissioner of the Freedmen's Bureau for Virginia, whom George Ben West asked to release the Casey Farm back to his father, was Colonel Orlando Brown, a surgeon of the 18th and 29th Massachusetts Infantry when the war began. He was stationed at Norfolk.

William Causey, one-time owner of Joe Wilson, a black man who was elected a Warwick County magistrate during Reconstruction, was a Warwick County farmer and owner of Causey's Mill, now part of Lake Maury of The Mariners' Museum.

Truck crops, widely raised by Newport News area farmers in the 19th century, were fresh vegetables. They were sent by schooners and larger ships to markets in Norfolk, Richmond, Baltimore, and elsewhere.

Captain Jerome Titlow, USA, of Lancaster County, Pa., was officer-of-the-day at Fort Monroe in 1865 when word came to shackle Jefferson Davis. He remained in Hampton after his Union military service was completed, and became sheriff of Elizabeth City County.

CHAPTER XI

Reconstruction Times

THE FACT THAT WE WERE SO CLOSE TO OLD POINT [Comfort] helped us in this section very much during Reconstruction times. The negroes did not care for the civil government but feared a U.S. soldier. When Sheriff [Jerome] Titlow had instructions to put the negroes off the Smith farm (and hearing that the negroes intended to resist), he summoned about 50 men as a posse, most of them without arms or ammunition as he thought the negroes, seeing this number, would submit. But they (the negroes) mustered nearly 200, armed with muskets they had gotten during the war, who took a fire position and ordered the sheriff back. When he refused, they fired, and nearly all the sheriff's men ran back to Hampton except for a few ex-Confederates who had pistols and shotguns and who returned the fire and then retreated.

Titlow went to the Fort [Monroe] and next day, with only a dozen or so soldiers, went on the farm and unroofed every shanty, and the negroes did not even protest. Yet the returned refugees suffered much indignity and humiliation, for they did not apply to the Fort, and if they had, would have been refused any assistance. The lands were occupied by the negroes, and they would not leave in many cases, and would not pay rent.

Mr. [George] Tunnel had bought a farm before the war from Mr. Powell, and as it was not paid for, Powell held a deed of trust. The wife and himself had died without children, and a slave, Nat, went out from Hampton and occupied the house and cultivated the farm, as Tunnel had refugeed with his family. Nat claimed the farm and Mr. Tunnel, when the war was over, had to build a log hut in the woods, and it was several years before he got his farm and house. Each individual had his own experience and trials, and as all who returned had enough to do to get something to eat and had no time for social intercourse, many things that transpired around us were known only to the parties to whom they happened. Each would have to give his own experience to tell the trials and sufferings that were borne by this community.

I made a crop of corn in '66, and got some rent, and we made out to get enough to keep from actual starving, but I am sure that neither father or Mammy Watson got such nourishment as their age and feeble systems required. The hard work in the day gave me not much time for thought, and the hard work produced profound slumbers, yet the gloomy look of the future, with not a ray of hope that things would improve, and to feel my inability to support the family as it should be, almost crushed me. I seemed utterly helpless. Father and Mammy were both of sunny and hopeful dispositions and did not utter a complaint but did all they could to cheer and encourage me.

Father and my cousin, George S. West, owned a tract of woodland called Gustwoods which father had kept in its original growth of pines till George should become of age. During the war a sawmill was placed near it, on the Briarfield farm. This mill was supposed to be run for the United States government, and they cut nearly all the pine timber off father's tract. George was living in Norfolk with his mother and young brother, Sheilds. He proposed in the fall of '66 to sell all the stave timber, as it was in demand and high, and for us to open a store in the house we lived in, and he would put an addition to a kitchen near the house for his mother and brother. This was done, and during the oyster season we did a very good business.

During this winter ('66 and '67) we began to feel that life was a pleasure. We had plenty to eat. After about five years of stinting and self-denials, we were not as economical as our yet limited means justified but were so much better off than we had been it was but natural we should indulge in luxuries we had been so long deprived of. We were quite happy and sanguine as to the future, though our surroundings and house comforts were yet very plain and crude. This was a very cold winter; the river was blocked with ice, and there were no communications with Norfolk for several weeks, so we had to get our goods from Hampton and haul them over in a cart. We had few religious privileges. As we had nothing but a cart to ride in to Hampton, so we could seldom get to church, and this was the case with the whole neighborhood.

In the spring a Sunday school was started, held in a house that had been built by Nick White on Ned Parrish's land where the road from Newport News and Jack Parrish's intersected with the county road to Hampton, (Twenty-fourth Street near Madison Avenue.) John F. Hawkins lived in it with his mother (both Baptists), and he was employed by White as a clerk in his store. John was made superintendent, and we had a very flourishing and interesting school. This was moved to the public schoolhouse, situated near the oil tank on the Causey farm, after the death of Mrs. Hawkins and the moving of John to Kentucky. I have forgotten who was the next superintendent, probably Henry Causey. This school was kept up as a union [interdenominational] school for some years. At the end of the war there was a negro Baptist church built on the Casey farm, near Roanoke Avenue and Twenty-second Street. This, in a year or two, moved on the Main Road on the Wilbern farm, about Warwick [Terminal] Avenue and Twenty-sixth Street, where it remained till it moved to its present site at Twenty-third and Jefferson Avenue.

In the spring of '67, while I was in Hampton, a U.S. marshal came over from Norfolk with one of the purchasers of father's Newport News farm and put the purchaser in possession, and he ordered father and George [George West, the author's cousin] to move at once and leave everything, both household goods and stock in store. They may have known that they did not intend to enforce this, or perhaps did not have the authority, though as yet we were under military rule and were subject to the will of a single man, to a great extent. On my getting home, everybody was in the highest state of excitement and consternation and hopelessness. We had just begun to feel that life was worth living and had become used to our rough mode of living, and now to lose everything and start again seemed impossible. We spent a horrible sleepless night; not a ray of hope in the awful gloom. I determined not to yield till forced to it. I knew that in law, possession was nine points.

The next morning I saddled my mule and went to Hampton to consult Colonel Mallory, father's lawyer. I found that he was in Yorktown, so I returned home. I started early the next morning and rode to Yorktown, saw Colonel Mallory, who said nothing could be done unless Major General John M. Schofield, then military governor of the State, would interfere, and advised me to see him and lay the case before him. General Schofield was then at the now Soldiers' Home [now Hampton Veterans' Administration Center], staying a short time.

I returned home that night and next morning went down [to Fort Monroe] to see the general and governor. He received me readily, and I had a long talk with him. I told him all the circumstances about our leaving home in '61, the age and condition of father, how I had taken possession of the house the year before, etc. He seemed to feel that it was a very hard case, and so expressed himself, but said he could not do anything for me as he had to obey the U.S. courts, and if the marshal asked for soldiers to put us out, he would be compelled to furnish them. I returned home very sad and almost hopeless.

That night we all assembled and discussed what was best to be done, and finally decided that if George and I could get a place in the neighborhood to continue storekeeping, that we should so do, as we were, we thought, making a living. A man named Williams was renting the Wilbern farm and was living in a small house built in the yard. On the place, near the Hawkins line, now between Thirty-first and Thirty-second street between West Avenue and the river, on the slope of the

After the war, freed slaves, categorized as contrabands before the 1863 Emancipation Proclamation, worked for wages with – and for – their former owners as well as the occupying U.S. Army.

ravine, was a barn and stable combined which had evidently been built by the Yankees during the war and was then, in '67, used as a sort of storage house by Mr. Williams. This was the only place we could get, and so we rented it at $5 a month. Father and the rest of our family moved again down to Mr. Turnbull's, who again took us in when we had not a place to lay our heads. George, Sheilds, and their mother [Aunt Eliza Tabb, widow of the author's uncle] took the room used for forage. We knocked out all the stalls in the stable part save one and made a store of this, and I slept in the vacant stall.

Aunt Eliza [Tabb] did the cooking for us. We moved all the goods and the household furniture, and no one tried to prevent us. We also worked and gathered the crops on the farm which we had already picked, but did not attempt to collect any rents from the negroes on the farm. The day we moved to the stable, I went to receive the goods and found the house overrun with rats, and they did not have anywhere to go as all the rubbish had been moved out. The house on the front was even with the ground, but on the back was up about ten feet on posts. While waiting for the loads I amused myself in shooting rats with a gun and killed a good many. That night we placed arsenic all about and killed immense quantities of them, and I think if any were left they went up to the Wilbern house, for we heard no more of them while there.

The odor of the stable we never got rid of, though Aunt Eliza kept everything very clean. We soon got used to our surroundings and made the best of our condition, hoping always for better things, Now, having time to think, we began to plan for the future. The ravine back of the house was a dense wilderness, particularly on the Hawkins land. We concluded to rent, if possible, a few acres from him, as Wilbern had sold his land. Mr. Hawkins agreed to let us have it without fixing a rental for it, saying that we would not fall out and that it wouldn't be much. As he and father had been very intimate all their lives except for a short time before the war, we concluded he did not intend to charge us anything, as with the exception of about an acre of arable land, the rest was hillside, and we had to so clear it up as to make his farm look a great deal better.

From this transaction I learned it is always best to have a definite understanding in all business transactions, for we leased the land for five years, and when we went to pay the rent at the end of the first year, Mr. Hawkins had become so convinced that we were doing well and his land was so valuable that he charged us $100 a year for it. We could not convince him this was too much, and as we had houses on it he had us in his power, so we waited, hoping he would compromise, and not till his death in 1870 did we get the matter fixed, when his heirs and we agreed upon the rent.

As I mentioned a disagreement between father and Mr. Hawkins, I will tell how it occurred. They had been intimate as boys and were really very fond of each other through life. Mr. Hawkins was a man very fond of young people, generous and hospitable, and his house was a most delightful place to visit, and during the summers was always filled with young men and ladies. He was a man of strong prejudices and a little envious. Having never had to work, having a fine farm and many negroes, and loving pleasure, he did not pay the strict attention to farming that some of his neighbors did, and so was not so successful. (I used to grieve to see him in his old age having to go out in the morning with his plow and work his crops.) A few years before the war someone bought up ship timber, and father, going in his woods, found out they were cutting on his land and learned that Mr. Hawkins claimed it. This brought on a lawsuit, a trial by jury that did not agree, and then the war.

The matter was never settled, but when Green was buying land around here for the now Old Dominion Land Company, we agreed if the railroad should come we would not lay any claim to it. We lost 24 acres back of the Casey farm, and Parrish lost 15 acres. The Casey farm fell short of the 24 acres, but Mr. Hawkins would not let his land be surveyed to see if he had more than his deed called for. William Ivy, the surveyor, was positive we lost the 24 acres. The war reconciled the differences between father and Mr. Hawkins. We rented from the river on the Wilbern line, running along this line to a short distance beyond the east side of West Avenue, and all the front of Mrs. [F. F.] Finch's except about 100 feet [on the] north.

During the summer and early fall, George and I, having little to do in the store during the day, cut down briars and bushes in the ravine and had a place leveled on the edge of the beach. We also cut a ditch through the ravine and had a road graded from the beach up the hill. George, being a good mechanic, with some assistance built a one-story store, 16 by 30 feet, on the place levelled about five feet above the beach, and on the hill above the ravine a two-story house, 16 by 24 feet. Both of these houses were weatherboarded with ¾-foot boards, and no plastering. We bought three negro shanties that were in the enclosure we made around the land we rented. One was good sized, and we used it in the summer for a kitchen. George and I had a room in the store, and father and the family moved on the hill.

Aunt Eliza married Samuel Lively and, with Sheilds, moved on the West farm owned by George, near New Market, about two miles from Hampton. We moved into our new quarters in November of '67, I think. We had the place enclosed, and the ravine, being now drained, made a nice pasture for a cow and range for chickens. We lived here till February 1870. During this time Mammy Watson died, and sister [Missouri] Sue married and moved to King and Queen County, and sister Lizzie and father lived alone. I became so lonesome for them, and father being frequently laid up with rheumatism, I decided to break up.

Henry Clay Whiting, Colonel Thomas Tabb, and a few others wished me to move to Hampton and open a private school, promising me their patronage, but as they would not guarantee a specific sum for my living, I was afraid to risk it. After awhile we decided to move to Richmond, since George had already gotten a clerkship in Norfolk. We moved into Mr. Marrow's house on Twenty-eighth Street near Clay Street [in Richmond] which he then rented. I found it quite hard to get a situation, and I had so little money from the sale of my goods that I did not see any openings to go into business.

Father was not as well satisfied [in Richmond] as while at Newport News. From the time of the restoration of the State courts till now, suit upon suit had been instituted against parties for whom he had gone security, and judgments had been obtained, and as in nearly every case the parties had lost everything, these judgments rested on father's land. The serving of these notices continually must have been very harassing to him, yet he was of so sanguine a nature and believed so much in the future of Newport News that while there he bore up and thought all things would come out all right.

He was not thinking so much for himself, but he wished to leave his children enough to keep them from so much drudgery.

About this time all these suits were consolidated and commissioners Mallory, Tabb, and Peek were appointed by the court to sell his lands and settle his affairs. A few years before this, father, by the advice of Colonel Mallory, finding he was on so much paper as security, had evidently given a deed of trust on his property to secure a few parties whom he individually owed, among them Mammy Watson, to whom he owed $1,000. When she died she left me all her property, having only very distant relatives. When the commissioners concluded to sell the Newport News farm at $100 an acre, I purchased the twelve acres next to the Burk farm, with a very small waterfront, believing they would run the lines from the river to the rear of the farm, which included the Pumpkin Hall tract. But they decided to run the lines only to the Newport News Creek, so that when the land was sold for sufficient to pay off all the debts, the heirs got the Pumpkin Hall tract without a waterfront instead of a slice near the center of the farm with water frontage.

Of course, I expected and did pay for it with what I received from Mammy Watson's estate. Father being away from Newport News, and having nothing to do—not even to think of my affairs and plan for me—and having very few visitors and not being able to go about on account of his blindness, for the first time I suppose in his life lost hope, and everything looked gloomy to him. All his property which had taken years of thought and labor to accumulate, and which had been so wisely selected as to look as if all his children would have a competency, was now it seemed about to be lost to them. He soon began to fail. I had secured a clerkship [in Richmond] on the wharf in the Virginia Steam Ship Company, but I determined to make an effort to return to Newport News.

After discussing the best plans, I decided to find out the purchaser of the Newport News farm at confiscation sale and try to purchase his interest in the twelve acres I had bought, for the confiscated interest terminated at the death of father, and as he was an old man I hoped to be able to get the twelve acres released for a small amount. It took some time to get the address, and when I wrote and asked what he would release it for, he was sick and did not answer, so that we thought he would do nothing; and father gave up again and gradually sank, the doctor said with no special disease.

He died December 8, 1871, and a few days after I received a letter from a lawyer in Washington stating that my letter to Mr. Alexander in reference to the purchase of his interest in the twelve acres had been referred to him after Mr. Alexander's death, and he wished to know what I would give, etc. I wrote him of the death of father and stated now the property was mine. I really believe, unless our days are numbered, that if early in the year I could have gotten possession and moved down, father's life would have been prolonged for years. How often have I wished that he could have seen the consummation of his prophecy that Newport News would become a great city. How he would have enjoyed seeing its growth and prosperity. But his work was ended, and he was called to enjoy the companionship of the Savior he so much loved. He had been a friend to all he came in contact with, and though he had been treated with indifference and ingratitude by those he befriended, yet I never knew him to complain or to refer to it, though it must have hurt him.

Though the house and land had been rented for the year 1872, yet I made arrangements and got possession and moved in the house in January and again opened store in the house. Sue, who then had two children, moved down in March, her husband not succeeding in King and Queen County, so I employed him. I only cultivated my twelve acres, but with the store made out to live quite well without going in debt to any extent. Though we had a good deal of company from Hampton, particularly young girls, for years we lived very happily and contented, even with our rough surroundings. I found out about the commissioners having run the line of the lots they sold only to the creek, and as I had so little frontage in comparison with the other lots, they agreed to sell me three more acres in a triangle, running back to my back line to a point.

The farm was bought by parties on speculation, believing that the Chesapeake and Ohio would make its deepwater terminus here. Mr. [A. B.] Green, an agent, had bought up a good deal of land but had very little waterfront. I now was living in hopes of the railroad and expecting my land to be very valuable when it came. After the death of Dr. Hope who had an eighth interest in 40 acres next to my 15 acres, I purchased his interest, as in the division I could claim and did get five acres next to mine.

Sue lost her oldest child in the summer of 1872, and she still continued to live with me, though her husband had returned to King and Queen County. All the wharves had become unfit for use or been carried away by ice, so that when we took a boat to Norfolk or Richmond we had to go out in a small boat, and then the steamer would stop and take on the passengers. I had a boat which I often used this way and also for pleasure and fishing, of which I was quite fond, and used to go quite frequently. My house was then in Elizabeth City County, the line running down the line of Burk farm and my northern line, and I had to go to Hampton to vote. Though for years it was useless as the negroes were in such majority and though I never was anything of a politician, yet I always went to vote just to show my opposition to the Republican party.

I served a good many years as judge of election. I will here record that the only cheating I ever saw in an election was tried by the Republicans, and that only once. I am sure that the negroes had as fair a chance to vote, without the least intimidation, as anyone ever had in this country. I did not, and do not now, believe that the negro ought to be entitled to vote, yet as judge I never questioned it if they had complied with the law. There was never anything like Ku Klux [Klan] or white caps down this way. Though the whites did not try to intimidate the negro, yet the negroes did force negroes to vote by threats of all sorts.

———————————

Beginning in 1893, the steamship **Pocahontas** *stopped in Newport News on its regular route between Norfolk and Richmond.*

SHERIFF JEROME TITLOW of Elizabeth City County was a former Federal army captain, originally from Lancaster County, Pa. After the Civil War he and many other Federal soldiers elected to remain on the Peninsula. They were known locally as "65ers."

George Tunnel, a farmer in Elizabeth City County who served in the Civil War, was a kinsman of George Ben West.

George Savage West was a cousin of George Ben West and the son of George Ben's deceased kinsman George West and his widow, Anna Elizabeth Smelts West. George Ben West's "Aunt Eliza" was beloved by the Parker West family and is frequently referred to in the memoirs. Mrs. West married secondly John Tabb and had a son, Sheilds Tabb, who married Sue Turnbull, all of Elizabeth City. Their sons were W. Lively Tabb, Benjamin West Tabb, and S. Bruce Tabb. B. West Tabb, named for George B. West, became vice president and treasurer of the University of Richmond. His daughter, Virginia Tabb, who married Roderick Dunn Moore, inherited the G. B. West manuscript and kindly made it available to the present editor.

Newport News' first Baptist Sunday school, which George Ben West helped organize in the late 1860s near the present Twenty-fourth Street and Madison Avenue, was the precursor of the First Baptist Church of Newport News, built in 1903.

The negro Baptist church built on the Casey farm at the end of the Civil War became the present First Church of Newport News Baptist. In 1972 its congregation moved to a structure at 2300 Wickham Avenue. The former church at Twenty-second and Jefferson was razed. The congregation is one of the oldest in the area.

Major General John M. Schofield, USA, was named military governor of Virginia, then U.S. Military District No. 1, shortly after Appomattox. He first governed from an office on the present Kecoughtan Veterans' Administration grounds at Hampton, site of a wartime Federal hospital, but soon moved to Richmond. In 1868–69 he became U.S. Secretary of War under President Andrew Johnson, and in 1888 commander of the U.S. Army.

Alexander B. Green came to Newport News about 1880 to buy up land for Collis P. Huntington. Some of this was utilized by the

Chesapeake and Ohio Railway, which began operating from Newport News to Richmond and westward in 1882. Other Huntington lands were administered by a holding company, the Old Dominion Land Company, chartered in 1880, which proceeded to develop a city and its needed utilities. Controlling interest in the Old Dominion was sold by Henry E. Huntington, Collis' nephew and trustee, to Newport News businessmen in 1925. The company was liquidated before World War II.

George Benjamin West's Aunt Eliza, widow successively of his uncle George West and of John Tabb, married as her third husband, about 1867, Samuel Lively of Elizabeth City County.

USA Maj. Gen. John M. Schofield

George Ben West after the Civil War rented farmland along the James, in addition to farming his father's remaining property. One from whom he rented was Mrs. Fenton Fielding Finch, the former Martha Melson. She was one of three heirs of John Hawkins, a major landholder who lived on the James near the later Thirty-fifth Street. When the Hawkins farm was divided after the Civil War in a partition suit between the three children of Indiana Hawkins Melson, daughter of John Hawkins, Mrs. Finch received the southerly one-third. This valuable property included much of later downtown Newport News, centering around Washington Avenue. The Finch estate in recent years passed through Anne Rebecca Finch Allaun, daughter of Martha Melson and Fenton Fielding Finch, to Mrs. Allaun's son, William E. Allaun Jr., Newport News attorney. Deriving originally from the Cole and Digges plantations of colonial Warwick County, the Hawkins-Melson-Finch-Allaun property remained longer in one line of descent than any other in Newport News.

George Benjamin West's youngest sister, Missouri (Sue) about 1870 married Robert Mortimer Smith. After having two children, they were divorced and Mrs. Smith spent the remainder of her life as hostess and housekeeper for her brother.

Henry Clay Whiting and Colonel Thomas Tabb, who wished West to establish a private school, were prominent Hamptonians.

Whiting was a merchant and Tabb an attorney.

Parker West in old age was harassed by claims against his lands by creditors of friends for whom he had secured loans before the Civil War, using his land as security. Through their failures he lost most of his land.

Attorneys Charles K. Mallory, Thomas Tabb, and G. M. Peek were appointed by the Elizabeth City County court about 1871 to sell the debt-encumbered farmlands of Parker West and to settle his affairs. After the settlement, West's heirs had only a small part of their pre-war holdings.

The Virginia Steamship Company, for which George Ben West clerked in Richmond briefly about 1871, operated the ship *Ariel* from Norfolk to Richmond, with stops at Newport News and other James River docks. The proper name of the company was the Virginia Navigation Company. The *Ariel* was succeeded by the *Pocahontas* in 1893.

Dr. Jesse P. Hope (1830–1893), who sold his interest in Newport News farmlands to George Benjamin West, was a Hampton physician.

"Sue," who lost her oldest child, Bell Howison Smith, in 1872, was George Ben West's sister, Missouri Parker Smith. She thereafter lived at her brother's house in Newport News and was divorced from her husband, Robert M. Smith.

George Ben West in 1872 was living on his remaining acres of the Parker West farm at approximately Seventeenth Street and River Road. About 1900 he built a house at the corner of Thirty-fourth Street and West Avenue, where he lived till he died in 1917.

Like most white Virginians of the post-Civil War era, West was Democratic and strongly anti-Republican in his politics. This grew from his opposition to Republican pro-Negro policies in the Civil War and Reconstruction. He was pleased when a Democrat, General Fitzhugh Lee, achieved the Virginia governorship in 1886. Thereafter Virginia's government remained in Democratic hands till the election of Linwood Holton, a Republican, as governor in 1970.

The Ku Klux Klan was organized by ex-Confederates in Tennessee in 1866 to maintain white supremacy and oppose Republican Reconstruction policies. The Knights of the White Camellia were a similar organization in the lower South.

CHAPTER XII

Old Dominion Land Company

FOR A GOOD MANY YEARS I HAD WORKING FOR ME a negro man, born free, who did not wish to lose the time to vote yet he told me he did not dare to stay away from the polls for fear the negroes would do him some harm. The negroes were very much upset by the [supposed] election of [Samuel J.] Tilden, [Democratic candidate in the Presidential election of 1876. Rutherford Hayes, Republican, was elected]. I think the most of them really believed, for they were so told by the Yankee carpetbaggers, that when the Democrats got in power after awhile the negroes would be again enslaved. I never tried to get a negro to vote, for I did not believe he ought to be allowed, nor did I ever but once discuss politics with a negro, and it occurred this way:

An old negro, Bob Anderson, rented part of the Casey farm. He was of more than ordinary intelligence, had been a foreman of his master, and had so behaved himself that he was highly thought of by all, negroes and whites. I was on the farm on business just after an election in which [General William] Mahone had been defeated. Bob asked me to give him some advice about the farm, and I referred him to Colonel Celey, who had been, as usual, very active in getting the negro vote out for Mahone. He said Colonel Celey did not know as much about this matter as I, so I gave him my opinion.

In a few moments he asked my opinion about a matter that I knew and he knew Colonel Celey would be the best judge of. So I again asked him why he didn't ask Colonel Celey, and he then admitted that in most matters he looked upon the Southern people as his best friends, and he could rely upon them more than the Yankees. Then I asked him why he did not do this when elections came off. I told him what was my interest was necessarily his. This he denied to be so in politics, so I then accused him and the negroes generally of being afraid of being put back into slavery. He admitted this to be a fact. He said he was so old he did not think he would ever be, but if the Democrats should again rule the country for any length of time, he thought his children or grandchildren would be enslaved.

But to return to Tilden's election. The negroes believing as they did were very much cast down and had very little to say about the election. When the [Congressional] Commission decided in favor of Hayes, they were jubilant. I slept in a front room without blinds, and I was awakened by a discharge of guns, and when I opened my eyes, the whole house seemed to be in a blaze. I looked out the window and saw a crowd of negroes around a pile of cornstalks they had brought down from the field above to make a bonfire. They began to cheer for Hayes and groan for Tilden. I was very mad, as the firing and fire had frightened me and all in the house, and I did a very foolish thing. I put on my pants and took my gun and went out and ordered them away from the premises. I found about 40 negroes, all armed with muskets but loaded only with blank cartridges, which they were firing. Fortunately, they were from the neighborhood and knew me well, and were doing this to celebrate their victory and to crow over me.

They did not become offended by my threats and belligerent attitude, but at the suggestion of a few of the older and wiser of them, at once left my land and very soon dispersed. I had always gotten on well with the negroes, and they not only then but always have looked upon me as a friend who would aid them if I could. And though I had very few neighbors but them, I lived during these years without the least fear and knew they would do me a favor with great pleasure and protect my crops and home in any way they could.

About 1879 there seemed to be a doubt of the C&O railway terminating here. A great deal of land had been bought in and around Yorktown and on the Piankatank [River], and as Mr. [Alexander B.] Green, who we supposed was an agent of theirs, did not buy (because he could not) any of the deepwater front, the prospects of a railroad looked gloomy. Even I, who had been so sure of a road that I had remained on the place, just making out to live until every one of our white neighbors had died or moved away, became a little doubtful and discouraged and had decided not to remain more than two years longer.

Green was the agent for what is now the Old Dominion Land Co., in which at that time, Mr. [Collis Potter] Huntington had no interest. Green called, in '79 or the first part of '80, a meeting at Barnes' Hotel in Hampton of all the owners of the waterfronts of the West farm to see if we could not make an offer to Mr. Huntington to induce him to bring the road to this point. He told of the advantages of other places and the inducements that they had offered and said unless the waterfront could be secured, the railroad would certainly go to some other place. The owners of the lots of the Newport News (father's) farm would not agree to sell. They still believed this to be the best place and wished to participate in the enhanced value of the lands when the road should come. But they agreed to lump the whole farm and divide it in half— they to have the half next to the creek at the point, and to sell the other half to Mr. Huntington for $100 an acre. (I am not sure as to the price.)

I would not agree to put my land in, as I considered mine much more valuable where it was than if nearer the creek [Newport News Creek], and so withdrew from the meeting.

After the conference and the proposition, Mr. Green came to me to see what I would do, and I told him if the road came I would give Mr. Huntington half of my 20 acres if he did not interfere with me in the possession of the other ten acres. He tried to get me to fix a price for all my land, saying they were able to pay for it and wanted all, but I would not yield. Mr. Huntington did not accept the proposition, and the road became more and more doubtful every day, until at last the owners became so discouraged and doubtful that they gave to Edward S. Hamlin, [a land speculator] who owned the Wilbern farm, an option to sell it at $300 an acre, all except the Whitehead and Tucker pieces which I think were in litigation; half acre of McDevitts, I believe; three acres of Kimberly's and five of Groome's in the 40-acre piece of which I bought Dr. Hope's share. At the same time, I gave what I had promised Green—an option to give half of mine when the road was a fixed fact with the proviso he was not to disturb me in my ten acres.

Some decision had been made in '76 in reference to confiscated property. I think it was in the case of McVeigh in Washington, where it was decided that only the life interest of the parties was taken, but the lawyers contended that father's debts were liens on it. As we did not wish that anyone should lose anything by father, even where he was only security, and as the property had only sold for enough to pay off these debts, we, the children, had taken no action looking to

West Avenue, Newport News' choice residential district of the 1890s, as shown in the 1892 Old Dominion Land Company promotional booklet, was one of several area developments created by the Old Dominion Land Co.

the recovery of the property.

After Mr. Huntington had accepted the options, he found out about the cloud on the title and sent a lawyer, Mr. Storrs, down to buy out our interest. Mr. Storrs became associated with Mr. Arthur Segar, a schoolmate of mine. They were very anxious not to let it be known that they were negotiating with us, as they said they feared they would lose the options. So our negotiations were very secret, and they asked that we mention it to no one. As I now think of it, they did not wish us to consult a lawyer. Arthur having been a schoolmate and being a friend, I thought would not be a party to taking any advantage of us. This shows how little I then knew about the duties and obligations of a lawyer to his client. I thought Arthur would act for me and in my interest as much as in the interest of Mr. Huntington, and I somewhat blamed him for not informing me of things that might have been to my advantage and keeping from me what would have helped, as we were some weeks in coming to an agreement.

At first I was disposed to charge about $100 an acre, but as we

By 1889, Newport News was growing rapidly north of the C&O terminals, part of which are shown in foreground. In the middle distance is the Warwick Hotel, built by the C&O, and beyond it, the shipyard.

did not wish any of those who held father on notes as security to lose anything, and as Huntington's lawyers agreed to pay (in addition to what they would pay us), enough to pay off all father's debts as well as enough to pay those who had bought the lots on speculation to cover what they had paid and interest, we thought Mr. Huntington would, after getting our right and title to the property, claim a good title and refuse to pay any money to those from whom he had gotten options. Should he put up such a claim and the courts decide in his favor, then without any expense to us we would receive the balance of the farm that Mr. Huntington had no option on—about 30 acres—which, when the railroad should come, would be worth more than the whole farm at that time. These lots which he could not secure an option on were five acres Whiting had sold to Mrs. Groom, three acres of Kimberly's, a half acre of McDevitt's, and 20½ acres of Whitehead's and Tucker's. So at last we signed our rights for $8,000, thinking we would eventually get these lots besides.

I have often wondered how it was that I, with such little business experience and without a single one to advise with who knew any more than I, should have been able to make even as good terms as I did and to retain the ten acres of land when I had such an unscrupulous man as Mr. Huntington to deal with. He had so much money and therefore power behind him, so I have always counted myself fortunate to have come off in all the condemnations and lawsuits with him as well as I did. I do not think I ever talked with him but twice. The first time in Lake's store in Hampton, the next time after they had begun the road and he and a party from New York came out to Newport News to inspect. The party was on the hill at the Burk house, and he sent for me and came out by himself to have the talk.

He told me frankly that I was in his way and he wished to buy me out. This was before any condemnation proceedings had been instituted. I informed him I had kept the land for a home and had no desire to sell, but I knew he had enough money to buy me out if he wished to. He then asked my price and I told him we would give up my ten acres, the Pumpkin Hall tract, and the Casey tract, for $100,000. He laughed at the price and said it was not worth one tenth of it. I told him I was perfectly willing and rather desired to hold it than to sell it at what I had named.

For some years after this there were rumors all through this section to the effect that I had been offered different prices for my land, some as high as the $100,000. I never was made an offer for my ten acres until Barrett and Vest accepted the offer I made them, though I expect there are few but yet believe I had good offers for it.

After Mr. Huntington got all the options he could, and the land company, I suppose, gave him a large interest in their lands, the C&O decided to make this their deep water terminus. During the fall of 1880 we were continually looking for the men to begin work. I think it was December 8, 1880 when Mr. [Walter] Post came with some wharf builders to start work. Soon after, they began to get piles. I rendered them every assistance in my power. They used the water from my spring for pile drivers, free of cost. They built some shanties on my beach and piled my whole waterfront with piles and lumber, and I did not even think of charging. I was but too glad to help all I could.

All the neighbors had left or died except Ned Ivy, who lived in what is now called the old house, just beyond his new house, and the Mourings at the old Jack Parrish house. Mr. Post, who had charge of the men for I. E. White, soon brought his wife down and occupied the Hawkins house, and John Guzzy and his bride lived in the house in Wilbern's yard. The house was occupied and had been for some years by Stephen

West and his wife and child, and by Mr. and Mrs. Potts and their daughter, but these were not congenial neighbors. Mr. R. A. Williams, and Arthur and his wife, moved into the Melson house, which was built very near the one I had torn down on the Hawkins (now Melson) property. So we soon began to get some very agreeable and congenial neighbors.

The treatment I received from the Yankees had so embittered me that up to this time I had never invited a Yankee in my house. John and George Blackmore, who had (or their father had) bought part of the Celey Smith farm, had tried to be friendly, and I had often talked to them in my yard but did not invite them on to the porch or into the house. I realized that I was treating them rudely, but I could not bear to give even color to the supposition that I thought them my equal socially. Remember that most of all Yankees who had been left behind in the wake of the army put themselves upon an equality with the negroes and were influencing the negroes to vote contrary to the interest of the Southern people, and really against their own interest, and put into office men who sought offices only to make the most out of them for their own pockets.

I have never yet gotten entirely over the feeling that a Yankee, on account of his peculiar teachings and bringing-up, is far inferior to the better class of Southern people. I do not believe the world ever saw or will ever again see, unless the millennium comes, such high state of civilization and culture and exalted virtue as was in the Southern states prior to the war. I have yet to find one Yankee, though I do not say there are none, who, when the money test is made, will not for his own interest do some small or little thing, and often mean thing, if it is to his advantage to do so.

Writing as I now do after the lapse of nearly 40 years (and years do soften, and old age ought to) one may somewhat judge my feeling about the Yankees when the war ended. I must say that I have not been thrown very much with them socially or in a business way, and also am very much prejudiced, so I do not even now wish to be too intimate either socially or in business. Still, feeling this way, it was a little pleasant and very desirable for the family to have these neighbors to visit, and we have kept up the intimacy somewhat. We soon began to get some very nice Southern families, and so we had a very agreeable change from our extreme isolation.

My two sisters living with me, of course, enjoyed more than I the privilege of visiting and being visited by agreeable people. They had been cut off from such intercourse for so long a time, and Lizzie, who was very social and cordial in her nature, missed more than the others by this isolation from friends and acquaintances and enjoyed immensely the advantages of this social visiting; she became very popular not only with her Southern but also her Northern friends.

I employed Richard Howard in 1881 to work the farm for me, but my business in the store increased so much and I began to rent out lots for parties to build on, that I did not do a great deal of farming and took him often into the store to help me. I think before the end of the year, or it may have been the next year, I employed Merriam on the recommendation of the Rev. J. J. Gravatt and found him to be a most excellent clerk. M. B. Crowell built a storehouse on the north side of the cut made from Pier 1 (now Pier 6) and had been appointed postmaster.

I think the post office was named Minnetta for an adopted daughter of Mr. Huntington. The name of the post office, different from Newport News, was very much criticized by the papers of the State, so that the Postmaster-General soon changed the name to Newport News. This discussion extended to why this point was named Newport News. James Barron Hope, an old Hampton boy and the editor of the *Norfolk Landmark*, had more perhaps than anyone else to do with the change of the name to Newport News. All his articles on the name showed research, and I think it was conceded by all the papers that his version of the derivation of the name was the proper one. I should really like to have preserved all of these articles, but I suppose the future historian of the city may be able to get hold of them. My impression now is that he claimed the name from Captain Newport, who here met the disheartened colonists who were fleeing on account of lack of food, and sickness, and were met here by Captain Newport. On account of the good news he brought, it was called Newport News Point.

Speaking of James Barron Hope, he told me about this time that he was collecting material for a history of this Peninsula, which he thought the greatest place on earth. He said it was a labor of love and that he was so busy that he feared he would not be able to write it before he died. I have often wished his daughter, Mrs. Marr, would continue the research and be able to give the world such a history. I was crossing Hampton Roads on a steamer, and he was talking to a party of Hamptonians, and he mentioned as a fact that the rich West

India islanders, in early colonial times, had handsome residences all along the roads from Hampton Creek to Newport News Point, and came up in the summer and lived there. I have no doubt he collected valuable information about the whole Peninsula.

I remember he also mentioned the fact that there had been a great battle fought by the colonists with the Indians at Newport News. I told him there was a curious formation on the river bank on the Wilbern farm that had always been called the Indian Fort, and he said no doubt that was the scene of the battle and that he would try and come over to Newport News sometime and investigate the locality, but he only lived a few years and never came. The fort still remains and is on the riverbank between Twenty-eighth, Twenty-ninth, and Thirtieth Streets, if they were extended to the river.

When the cut from Pier 1 (now Pier 6) was widened, Mr. Crowell moved his store to the northeast corner of Twenty-third and West Avenue, and it afterward burned down. This moving was before the cut was made for now Pier 5 (formerly Pier 2), and there was no obstruction by the coal dock, it not being built. In the spring of '81, Mr. C. W. Newman of Madison County leased a lot from me and put up quite a large building to be used for a hotel. He was quite active in the Baptist church and gave his dining room up on Sunday evenings for church services. His wife had consumption and he had soon to leave for the Red Sulphur Springs for her health. They had a daughter about eight or nine years old. Dr. Garnett rented it and came over from Norfolk to practice here. Mrs. Garnett afterwards bought the house, and it is now owned by Williamson. Dr. Joseph Charles was the next physician here and learned a great deal from Dr. Garnett, who, though a fine doctor, drank and could not be relied on. The Garnett family was a great addition to our list of friends.

I became involved in lawsuits with Huntington about the division of the 20 acres, and with the railroad, which instituted a suit to run a track down through the ten acres and also across my waterfront to get the riparian rights. I did not know how to lay off my land, so I used the road I took to go out to the public road to Hampton, and leased lots facing on it. Part of this road was on me and part on the C&O (formerly Burk farm.) In a short while the railroad also rented land facing this road, and in a few years there was quite a street of shanties on either side and nearby. Nearly all (at least four-fifths) of the town was over there.

IN THE DISPUTED presidential election of 1876, Democrat Samuel J. Tilden was first declared winner. However, an election commission named by Congress decided disputed elections in South Carolina, Florida, Louisiana, and Oregon in favor of Republican Rutherford Hayes, assuring Hayes' election.

"Carpetbaggers" were Northern adventurers who came south to gain money and power in Reconstruction. They carried their possessions in carpetbags.

General William Mahone, CSA, was active in Virginia politics from Reconstruction until his death in 1895. He successfully advocated the "readjustment" of Virginia's wartime bonded debt, creating a Readjuster party of populist character which aided the Republicans. Mahone's protegé, William E. Cameron, was Readjuster governor of Virginia from 1882 to 1886, and Mahone was United States senator from Virginia from 1881 to 1887.

The presence on the lower Peninsula after the Civil War of masses of unemployed blacks created serious problems. One area was called "Bloodfield" because

CSA Gen. William Mahone

of its violence. After white residents moved from Eighteenth Street about 1900 to streets further uptown (as George Ben West himself did), that area became a raffish mixture of waterfront saloons, houses of prostitution, and black rental property, known for its violence as "Hell's Half Acre." As the employment opportunities and literacy of blacks improved in the twentieth century, their social condition improved.

Collis Huntington in the 1870s considered sites in Norfolk, Mathews County, Middlesex County, Yorktown, and elsewhere before choosing Newport News for his rail terminus.

James H. Storrs of Brooklyn, an attorney for Collis Huntington, was an incorporator of the Huntington holding company, the Old

Dominion Land Company, in 1880. He was a director of the firm, and his son Frank was its secretary.

Arthur Simkins Segar (1844–1901) was a Newport News attorney whose clients included the shipyard and Chesapeake and Ohio Railway. Unlike his uncle Joseph Segar of Hampton, who was a Union sympathizer, he went with his State and served in the Confederate Army. He is buried in St. John's churchyard, Hampton.

Lake's store, where George Ben West first met Collis Huntington, was on Queen Street, Hampton. It was the property of John L. Lake, who dealt in real estate and owned Lake's brick block, near St. John's Church.

Barrett and Vest, who accepted George Ben West's offer and bought his remaining acres of Newport News farm, were William E. Barrett, an attorney who married West's niece, Emily Smith, and William B. Vest, a banker who married another niece, Bettie Marrow.

Walter Post, who came to Newport News in 1880 to direct construction of the Chesapeake and Ohio, became manager of the Newport News Shipbuilding and Dry Dock Company in 1905 and president in 1907. Post Street in Hilton Village, a Warwick County housing development now part of Newport News, was named for him. He was Newport News' first mayor, in 1896–98.

Walter Post, a C&O official, became Newport News' first mayor in 1896.

"Ned" Ivy, or E. T. Ivy, owned a farm between Newport News Creek and Salter's Creek, fronting Hampton Roads. He was the son of William Ivy, a surveyor.

The Blackmore property adjoined Salter's Creek and Hampton Roads. A plat dated July 1878 shows it contained 88 acres of high ground and 44½ acres of marsh. It had been earlier a part of Celey's plantation, acquired by Major Thomas Celey in the 17th century and deeded by his son Thomas to Colonel William Wilson in 1695. Wilson's daughter Mary, who inherited the plantation, successively married William Roscow, Colonel Miles Cary, and Dr. Archibald Blair, the latter of Williamsburg. A brick house which stood close to the present Mary Immaculate Hospital site was destroyed in the 19th century.

West's sisters living with him were Elizabeth Roberta West and Missouri West Smith, or Sue.

The Rev. John J. Gravatt was rector of St. John's Church, Hampton, from 1876 to 1893.

A larger post office was opened at Newport News in 1881 and the site named Minnetta in honor of a relative of Collis Huntington. It was soon redesignated "Newport News" in response to public demand. Shortly thereafter, 1882, the area was cut off of Elizabeth City County, by act of the General Assembly, and joined to Warwick. In 1888 the village became the county seat of Warwick, the county courts being moved from Denbigh to a new courthouse at Twenty-fifth Street and Lafayette (later Huntington) in Newport News. In 1896 the community was chartered as a city, and the Warwick County seat was then returned to the former courthouse at Denbigh.

James Barron Hope, founder and editor of the *Norfolk Landmark* and well-known poet, was a native of Hampton. He read commemorative poems for the 250th anniversary of Jamestown's settlement in 1857 and at the 100th anniversary of the Yorktown surrender in 1881, both later published. His daughter was Mrs. Jane Hope Marr, wife of Colonel Robert Marr of Virginia Polytechnic Institute.

Derivation of the name "Newport News" was long disputed, as George Ben West indicates. Research confirms that it was early given to the point of land on the James where departing Jamestown colonists, after the Starving Time of 1610, encountered Christopher Newport's supply ship arriving from London and turned back to continue the Virginia settlement.

On behalf of his sisters and himself, George Ben West in 1886 brought suit against Collis Huntington to recover title to Newport News farm, which commissioners had sold in the 1870s to satisfy claims against Parker West's estate. The suit was carried to the Supreme Court of Virginia but failed. However, George Ben West and his sisters still held 15 acres inherited from his father's Newport News farm plus the 60-acre Pumpkin Hall tract and 214-acre Casey farm in Newport News' East End. These brought them wealth.

CHAPTER XIII

My Past Life

ON OCTOBER 19, 1881, THERE BEING A CELEBRATION at Yorktown to commemorate the surrender of Cornwallis, an excursion train was run [by the Chesapeake and Ohio] from here [Newport News]. A large party came over in a boat from Smithfield, and we started at 9 o'clock in the morning. Just beyond the Lee Hall house there had been laid a branch [rail] road to Yorktown. We arrived at the National Cemetery in Yorktown at 1 o'clock in the afternoon, and quite a force was putting down rails and ties to extend the road to the Moore house. I do not think the road was used after that day, or was used beyond the cemetery. We carried our dinners and picnicked near where the cars stopped. We arrived too late for the grand parade that day. We took the cars at the same place at about 6, and arrived at home about 11 p.m. I think there was an excursion from Richmond by the C&O the same day, so that was probably the first time passengers could have gone from Newport News to Richmond on the C&O railroad. I remember that night the bushes striking against the car window when we passed through cuts. The putting down of this branch was a financial failure, and the track was soon taken up.

The latter part of October I went up to the State Fair at Richmond. I am sure there were no passenger cars running at this time; had there been I would have gone by them and not by boat. I stayed four or five days and I think I returned November 2 or 3 by [railway] car to Newport News. I do not know it to be a fact, but I believe I was the first pay passenger who came through from Richmond to Newport News. We left Richmond at 9 p.m. with a dozen or more, mostly from Williamsburg, and when they got off I was the only passenger. Knowing I had to spend the night on the car, I borrowed a blanket from my sister, and after leaving Williamsburg got so soundly asleep that I did not awaken until the conductor informed me we were at Newport News. This was after 4 a.m.

The C&O railroad ran down the main street of Williamsburg. There was no passenger depot here then, [in Newport News] and the first depot was in No. 1 Pier (now No. 6), and afterward in Pier No. 2 (now No. 5.)

I commenced this writing three or four years ago, and often did not write for weeks, and sometimes only a very little a day, so that I was probably nearly two years in writing. I have not written anything for over a year, but I think I will now (August 1903) write some more. The way I have written necessarily makes me record things not in order but just as they come to my mind. I have not had a single memorandum but have had to rely entirely on my memory. In looking back at my past life, it has often occurred to me how little [a part] I have had in the shaping of my course, and how different my life has been from what I thought it would be when I was growing up. I think that perhaps every boy should decide what he intends to make of himself as soon as possible, and I have often advised boys to do so. And yet, there so often takes place things we cannot foresee that will change entirely the course of one's life, that it would seem useless and hopeless for one to mark out what he intends to do. Still, everyone should have a purpose in life and should follow it as much as possible, but not to the extent that he could not be swerved from it no matter what occurs, but rather to be and to do such and such things if providence does not oppose, but rather opens the way to the accomplishment of what he sets out to do.

God rules, and we should put ourselves in His hands and be willing to do whatever it seems that He would have us to do. But how few young people are willing to do this. In their youth and strength they think they can do anything they will, and though the leadings of providence may seem to lead another way, they will not follow but rather resist, and sometimes make wrecks of their lives and become failures in life. I have been led to write this because of the fact that I had no definite purpose of what I should do or be when I was growing up. Now, looking back over so many years (and so many seemed to have been wasted), it does seem to me that if I had determined on some course and had tried to follow it that perhaps I should have accomplished more and been of more use to my fellow men than I have been.

Yet, I believe that God has been my guide and helper and has so ruled and guided that perhaps the very years that I now consider wasted or useless may have been, and I sometimes think were, a schooling preparing me for the accomplishment of some of God's purposes, and I hope this is so and that my life has not been altogether useless, but may be or has been for His glory and the betterment of mankind. I know and feel how little I have done, but yet if I have been faithful even a little, and have done His will only a few times, let Him have all the glory and the short time that remains for me on earth, may I seek more and more to know His will and be guided by His Spirit and be faithful to Him and my fellow men. May my life be devoted to Him, and may it glorify His great and Holy Name. This is the chief purpose of our being brought into the world, but how few accomplish it and how little these even do. Let me only remember the past and its shortcomings and failures to make me more zealous to do His will in the future.

May I, as the Israelites of old, be continually reminded of what God has done for me all along through life, and above all, the hope I have by His grace through faith in His Son of the blessed inheritance in the Promised Land. He, who has suffered so much and has died as a propitiation for me, should have my whole life, and He has bestowed [it] upon me, for I am not my own but have been bought with a great price. May He who sits now at the right hand of the Father claim me as His own. What can I withhold from Him who has done so much for me and of whom I hope and expect greater things? Bless the Lord, O my soul, and all that is within me, bless His holy name. Bless the Lord, O my soul, and forget not all His benefits. What shall I render unto the Lord for all his benefits towards me?

I suppose if anyone were to ask those who know me, they would say I have had a successful life. I have had for many years enough means to satisfy all my wants, and the prospect bright for the future. My home life has always been happy, my health has been good. And yet, I know of so many failures and shortcomings, I have done so many things I ought not to have done and left undone so many things that I ought to have done. And there is no good in me.

My early years were surrounded with all the blessings that the most exacting might wish. My father had begun to accumulate property, was a successful farmer and was making money. My father, mother, and Mammy were Christians—loving, affectionate, kind—as were my brother and sisters. I was perhaps as much spoiled and petted as anyone could be, yet I was taught to mind and to know what was meant when I was told *no*. I was waited upon and petted, even by the servants, and to such an extent that I was not made to do as much as I ought and grew up very indolent and lazy. I early became fond of study, and had I had proper teachers would have acquired a good education.

I have mentioned that I was sent to [Colonel John B.] Cary at six years, not knowing my ABCs. He then taught in what was called the Old Courthouse in Hampton, back of the Courthouse, near the [fire] engine house. He was not, at this time, a suitable teacher for one so young, though I learned because Mammy Watson always saw that I was prepared before I left for school. At the end of two sessions, Cary took charge of the academy (somewhat a free school). Father, believing that only persons should be sent to it who could not afford to pay tuition, took us away. I do not know how Cary was paid, but suppose he received a salary to teach boys and girls whose parents were unable to pay, and tuition from those who were able to pay. I then went to private schools for a few years, but they did not amount to much, and I believe every year we had a new teacher. After this, free schools were established in all the county. I suppose they were kept up by taxation as now, for father sent me to them instead of to Cary at the academy.

All of these years were wasted, for the teachers were, I suppose, such as could do nothing else. They had no order and were indifferent to whether or not the scholars learned. Frequent changes were made in teachers. I did little studying and took to reading weekly papers, with continued stories, and mostly sensational and trashy. I kept up and stood well in my classes but had no incentive to learn.

Mr. Cary having built an academy of his own, in the session of '55 and '56, I again went to him. This academy was near the other but faced the water—a beautiful situation and now occupied by Dr. James T. Boutelle, the Baptist parsonage, Jesse Jones, and a house built by James McMenamin. Cary also built quite a large dwelling and kept boarders; the boys slept in the third story of the academy, the girls in his house, and all ate in his dwelling. I was put in the classes of some boys about my age but was not as well prepared as those who had continued with and been taught by Cary. I found it very hard at first to come down to hard study, but never liking to be near the foot of the class and always striving to be at the head, after awhile I got into traces and was able to be at least next to the head. I remained till the session of '59 and '60.

The first two years at Cary's I studied hard, but the last year did very little. I have mentioned that I took too many and too high classes at the University [of Virginia]. The first year I graduated in math, which I was always fond of and which was much easier to me than the languages. I have always been sorry that I did not take literature instead of modern language—French and German. They did not then as now pay so much attention to English, which I now think was a great mistake. The next session I could not or did not study; there was too much discussion of secession and war. I left before the end of session.

The war came on, and I have not done any real studying since '60. When the war was ended, I could have gone, and perhaps would have gone, to work that was more congenial and for which I was better fitted than farming, but father was blind and Mammy Watson old, and father's affairs were in such condition that someone had to look after them, and it was my duty to think more after the comfort, pleasure, and welfare of my family than of engaging in congenial business and trying to prepare myself for any kind of life work.

After the death of Mammy Watson and father, my mind was not inclined to any special business, and owning the 15 acres I had bought of the Newport News farm, and believing the C&O would certainly make its terminus here, I made up my mind to wait for it, believing that when the road came that the advance price of land would make me comfortably off. I had lost, if I ever had any, my ambition to be wealthy or even to be what the world calls very successful in life.

When a child, like all children, I had a very erroneous idea of life, and as father seemed to have almost as much as anyone in this section, I considered him rich and if I thought at all, I thought that I would have enough to live on, and it was not necessary for me to mark out any special thing that I should be. Father's idea was that I should get a good liberal education, and then I would be fitted to take up any profession or business that I might desire to engage in. This is contrary to the popular idea now, which is to specialize. I am of father's opinion.

The war coming on, I saw that what father had been working hard to accumulate for nearly 40 years was swept away—not by any fault of

The waterfront of Parker West's old farm looked like this in 1891, after the C&O had built piers and a tall grain elevator there.

his, or by any mismanagement, and that wealth had truly wings and could fly away. I then took another view and thought we had better enjoy the present and not to be laying up for a rainy day. My aspirations were considerably lessened. On my trip from Greensboro to Richmond, returning after [Lee's] surrender, probably in Pittsylvania County, we passed many one-story log houses with two or three rooms, nicely whitewashed and with a few shrubs or vines about them, and as I was returning to lands without a vestige of a house, I often thought I would be supremely happy if I was returning to a home as lowly as even these.

And when we took possession of the storehouse in '66, though the lower story had to be used as a crib, stable, wood house, etc., yet I was very thankful for even this, and well contented till we were driven out in '67. I was almost compelled to do some farming and also to keep store, and though I did not like either business much and do not think I would ever have made a good farmer or successful merchant, yet I tried to do the best I could under the circumstances and did learn a good deal of both farming and also merchandising. But I do not like either.

In '79 and '80 the prospect of the railroad terminating here became very gloomy, and as our neighbors had either died or moved away, it became very lonesome and undesirable a place to live in. I am sure that had the decision to bring the road here been delayed another year, I should have moved away. I had decided to become a surveyor because William Ivy was getting old and Ned [Edward A.] Semple was not as accurate as he ought to have been, and I was convinced that I could get some work to do. It took me only a short while to get back my knowledge of the theory, and by taking Mr. Ivy's notes I found out I could work out the acreage of land as well as he. So, in January of 1881 went with him to survey several pieces of land so as to get the use of the instrument. He always used a compass but was very accurate with it. I worked with him till I was convinced that the [rail] road would come and then, when my store business increased, I gave it up.

The town of Newport News grew up around the C&O piers near the former farms of George Ben West's family and their neighbors.

THE FEDERAL and Virginia governments jointly celebrated the 100th anniversary of Cornwallis' surrender at Yorktown in a three-day gathering October 18–20, 1881. Collis Huntington had promised officials that the Chesapeake and Ohio Railway would convey them by rail to Yorktown. Accordingly, rail crews worked night and day to lay temporary tracks down Williamsburg's Duke of Gloucester Street and thence via Lee Hall to Yorktown. Other C&O excursion trains went from Newport News via Lee Hall to Yorktown, where President Chester Arthur on October 19 laid the cornerstone for the Victory Monument in the presence of 20,000 people. The temporary spur track from Lee Hall to Yorktown was torn up soon after the Centennial, and the C&O tracks through Williamsburg were relaid north of that town. Regular C&O passenger service between Newport News and Richmond did not begin until May 1882.

The first C&O passenger stop in Newport News was at Pier 1, later renumbered Pier 6, at Eighteenth Street. A depot was later built at Twenty-second Street and the James River, which was taken over by Amtrak in 1972 when it absorbed the C&O's passenger service.

George Ben West began his memoirs in 1899 when he was 60. He continued them spasmodically until 1906. He resumed writing this segment in August 1903 after a lapse of a year. At that time he was 64 and president of the Citizens and Marine Bank, which he had founded in 1891. His memoirs reflect gratitude for his health and prosperity.

George Ben West in his views here expressed illustrates the reluctance of many Virginians to send their children to public schools, which originated in most areas in 1870 under terms of the Virginia constitution drafted by the Convention of 1868-9. Many Virginians felt that public schools were a device of Radical Republicans and Negroes to elevate blacks and gradually to mix the races. Nevertheless, the public school system rapidly took root after 1872 in Newport News and other Virginia localities.

The academy taught by John B. Cary at Hampton in 1855-56 was on Hampton Creek near Hampton Bridge, not far from Queen Street. Among occupants of the area in 1903 when West wrote these pages were Dr. James Boutelle (1856–1913), well-known physician and surgeon, and James McMenamin (1847–1901), founder of a crab-packing business. The section has since been cleared as part of Hampton's redevelopment. The waterfront street at the academy site was called Cary Street.

William Ivy and Ned [Edward Armistead] Semple were surveyors in Newport News and Warwick County. Semple (1842–1910) was born at Sherwood, the Booker family plantation on the present Langley Air Force Base grounds. He was the son of Dr. George William Semple and Emily Booker Semple. A civil engineer, he served as Elizabeth City County surveyor. His maps and papers are in the Virginia State Library.

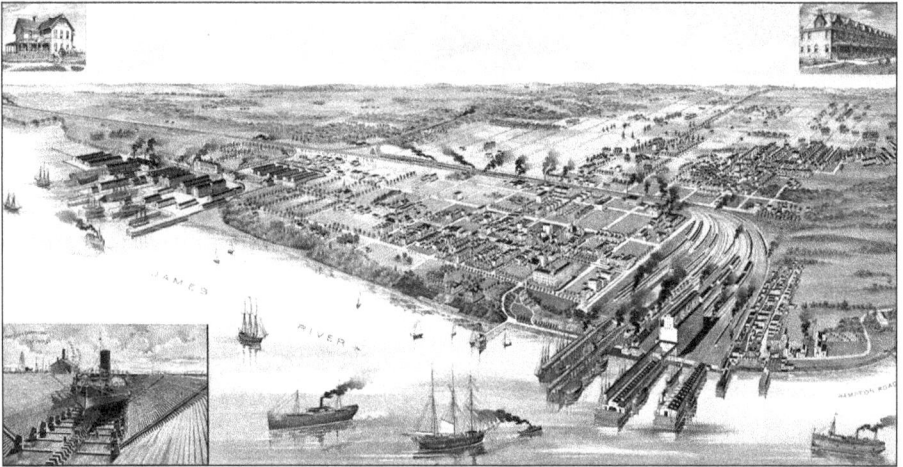

An aerial view of Newport News in 1891. Notice the grain elevator and the extensive railroad tracks and piers of the C&O (bottom right), as well as the shipyard piers further north (left). Tiny corner images show the drydock and new residential developments.

CHAPTER XIV

Looking Back

LOOKING BACK AT MY LIFE, IT NOW SEEMS TO ME that I was better fitted to be a civil engineer than anything else. I believe now I would have made quite a good one and I think the work would have been congenial to me. Had I gotten a position in the Engineering Corps during the war, instead of in the Quartermaster Corps, my whole course of life, I am sure, would have been changed. Whether for the better I know not, but I think not.

This is why I engaged in banking. After the death of Lizzie [West, his sister], I employed Eugene Turnbull to clerk for me, hoping he would take an interest and build up a business, so I could turn it over to him. This did not turn out as I hoped and now, as I was getting enough to support me from rents, and not liking storekeeping, I gave up the business. Then Fil Turnbull, who knew a good deal about the tinning business, wished to engage in it here, so I put up the money to start it and I also attended to the financial part, keeping books and paying bills, but I was not required to wait on store, yet I often did so. We were to divide the profits. We ran it for some time, but eventually it played out, and I did not receive the money back that I invested.

Willie Vest, who had been in the Planters' Bank of Richmond for several years and was not satisfied because others were promoted over him, asked me to see George Schmelz, who had established a private bank here, to give him a position. Willie had never been strong and healthy and seemed to be much better when he made visits to this section and was very fond of the water, fishing, etc., and wished to move down. George gave me no encouragement that he would give him a situation. A year or two before, Lem Hoskins

Sclater of Hampton had advised me to go into the banking business, but as I knew nothing about it, I gave his suggestion little thought. But now it occurred to me that Willie knew the business and that it might be well to start.

Mrs. Marrow and I had sold the Casey farm, and we would be receiving payments for it and could thus put in a good sum to start with. Willie [Vest] seemed delighted when I proposed to him to start a bank. It took but little time to get all the stock taken. I was very much gratified to find that so many people were willing to put in their money in an enterprise with me at its head, who knew nothing about it. I do not think there were over four persons I asked who refused to take some stock. I am gratified also to know that the confidence reposed in me was not misplaced and that all have been pleased with our management.

Since General [Nelson] Miles has been retired, and his unpopularity with the administration at Washington [made public], the matter of his treatment of President Davis—especially the order placing irons on him—has been much written about. I now recall to memory an interview I had with him

CSA President Jefferson Davis was imprisoned in Hampton's Fortress Monroe after his capture.

at Old Point. I had long since forgotten that it was with General Miles, but as he was the commandant [of Fort Monroe] while the President [Jefferson Davis] was imprisoned, he must be the man. Being in the Confederate government employ during the war, I learned something of the workings of the departments and learned it was always best to go to the head of departments if you wished anything done. I have mentioned how father's property was confiscated and the difficulty in recovering it.

I wrote a letter to the President of the United States, telling him of the treatment he [father] had received, and asking him to intervene on his behalf. I received a reply telling me to go to the fort [Monroe] and consult with the commander and that he had been ordered to investigate the matter. Enclosed was also an order to see the General [Miles]. As Mr. Davis was there, no one was allowed in the fort except on special permit. I remember how indignant I felt when I was sent by the corporal of the guard at the main gate, with an armed soldier on either side, to the office of the commander across the fort. I remember very little about the conference. He asked a few questions but in a way that impressed me that he did not sympathize with us, and I left fully satisfied that I had accomplished nothing, which was a fact, for I do not think he ever looked again into the matter. I would really like to see the report he made.

The contrast between the interviews with General [John M.] Schofield and him were very marked. The manner and words of General Schofield showed that he felt a great injustice had been done father whereas General Miles seemed to take it for granted that father was receiving only such treatment as he deserved. In this matter of shackling Mr. Davis, I believe he (Miles) was guilty of everything he has been accused of, but I also believe that Captain Titlow, when he executed the command [to shackle Davis] thought that he was doing an act for which he would receive honor, and I have no doubt for years he bragged about it. Titlow lived here for many years after, and I knew him, and he did not possess the instincts of a gentleman but was a rough and rude fellow and one I believe could be brutal. On a jury at one time, just after civil government was established and when Billy Wood was sheriff [of Elizabeth City County], he accused Titlow of stealing some things from his farm during the war. I believe Titlow was a willing tool in General Miles' hands.

While Mr. Davis was in the fort, Dr. [George] Woodbridge of Richmond, and Dr. [Otto] Barten of Norfolk, both Episcopal ministers, got a permit to visit him and started from Norfolk in the morning on the Richmond boat, to go to Old Point. For some reason, the boat did not go to the Point that day and Captain [Z. C.]Gifford of the steamer persuaded them to land here [at Newport News] and get me to carry them over to the Point. George West and I were getting ready to go to Hampton when they landed. We had nothing better than a cart to ride in, so another plank was put across the cart for these distinguished ministers to ride on.

What a picture we made when jogging along behind the white mule. It would now be very amusing, but then it showed too well what the South was reduced to. I am sure, though I had many such experiences, that it was their first and I hope last. I remember they were very jovial and kept George and me laughing most of the time, and I really enjoyed the ride. Dr. Woodbridge had a military air about him, and Dr. Barten was a fine, distinguished-looking man. Both looked very dignified, which did not at all correspond with the situation. I never met them afterwards. They got a better conveyance in Hampton to carry them to the fort.

I had had in the fall of 63 another furlough and came down [from Richmond] to Burwell's Bay [on the James, adjoining Isle of Wight County] to visit a Signal Corps in charge of Henry Causey and composed of Nat Gammel, Dick Hawkins, Lewis Davis, and some others. They crossed the river in a boat and landed about Deep Creek [in Warwick County, now midtown Newport News] and got such information as they could from the farmers they could trust about what was going on at Old Point. They always went at night and returned before day. They lived remarkably well, as they could get many of the luxuries from this side [i.e., the north side of the James], and there was plenty of game around them.

I remember one morning before breakfast some of the boys brought in a wild turkey and four or five large black wild ducks. I enjoyed the rest and quiet very much. I was not well and did not cross the river with them or even go hunting. The next year they were surprised [by Federal troops] and Lewis Davis was shot and captured and died of his wounds while in prison. I had to ride from the [Burwell's] bay to the Norfolk and Western Railroad [through Isle of Wight County] to take cars for Petersburg, on horse. I had not been on a horse for many years, and this was a very poor saddle horse, and I got a very severe jolting. As there was no [train] connection, I had to remain in Petersburg at a hotel that night. I could hardly walk, and it was painful to sit down. I had several blood boils after this trip.

Sometime during the war, one of our privateers, CSS *Florida*, contrary to international law, was taken in one of the harbors in Central or South America, and brought to this place [Newport News]. The

The USS Cumberland *is struck and eventually sunk by the CSS* Virginia *in Hampton Roads on March 8, 1862.*

great powers were about to make the United States put her back in the same place and restore her to our government, but she was sunk just off what is now [Chesapeake and Ohio] Pier 1 or 2, on this [the north] side of the [James River] channel. The United States claimed she was run into and sunk, but many believed she was scuttled and sunk, or at least run into by orders. After the war she was stripped by divers, and I have often been out over her to see the diving. She must have been magnificently built, for the divers said the staterooms were very handsomely decorated. I saw a piece of the gunwale which seemed to me to be of mahogany, and I have also seen brass ornaments which decorated the staterooms.

The [U.S. sloop of war] *Cumberland* was sunk by the [CS ironclad ram] *Virginia* off Pier 6, about the middle of the channel. The [US frigate] *Congress* in the fight was anchored a little lower down the river and on the other side of the channel. Her cable was cut, and she ran ashore on this side of the channel, just opposite what is now called Dawson City, this side [west] of Newport News Creek. I have very often been on the boats that worked on the *Cumberland,* first by a German named West and then by a company of Detroit, Michigan, which purchased her from West and which brought down a great many of the [Great] Lakes divers to try to secure the $40,000 in gold said to be in an iron chest in the paymaster's stateroom. I have also seen wreckers working on the *Congress* and have fished around her.

The way I found out the first location of the *Congress* in the fight was this. A small schooner, some years after the war, anchored just below where I live and kept store at the foot of Eighteenth Street. A very heavy storm came up and blew her across the channel, dragging her anchors. When the captain went to pull up anchor, he found with his crew he could not raise them. He came ashore to inquire if there was a wreck there and to get additional force to get up anchors. He hired some men and found he was into a chain, a good deal of which he pulled into his boat. He went to Norfolk and chartered another schooner and with the two, swung the anchor between them and carried it to Norfolk. The anchor proved to belong to the *Congress*. The cable had been cut when the *Virginia*, after sinking the *Cumberland*, headed for her.

I have been unable to find anyone—negro or white—who witnessed the fight between the *Monitor* and *Virginia* in Hampton Roads. Mrs. Ann Davis, who was living at Captain Wilbern's, her grandfather's, saw the fight with the *Cumberland* and *Congress* being in full view, and she saw the smoke of the fight with the *Monitor*, but cannot locate the exact place. She thinks it was just below the [Middle Ground] lighthouse, perhaps opposite the Ned Parrish place, but I think it was nearer Old Point.

After the sinking of the *Cumberland*, I understand the government tried to raise her, though she was sunk in a very deep hole in the channel. The paymaster, I understand, had $40,000 in gold with which to pay off the fleet, and this amount was allowed as lost in his settlement with the government. I understand she was raised to near the surface between boats; then the beams holding her broke, and she went down again. The German (West) bought her from the government with the guarantee the gold was aboard, and he worked for several years to get to the safe. I understood that if he should get the paymaster's safe and the money was not in it that the government would sue the men on the bond of the paymaster and make it good to West.

His plan, as told to me, was to start under the stern, which lay down the river, and blow a hole in her and work towards the paymaster's stateroom. He did the diving himself and did not attempt to get any wreckage save the pieces he blew out of the side and brought up on deck, and the copper bolts cut out.

The difficulty he had was the filling-in of mud and sand, and having to grope in the utter darkness. It was very dangerous, and several times he was brought up unconscious. He sold out to a company in Detroit which brought several deepwater divers in, and their plan was to send a diver down on the deck as near as possible over the stateroom. He was to cut a hole in the deck, let down a ladder to the next deck, put down another diver, cut another hole, send down another diver, and so on. They, too, failed.

One of the company, a Mr. Smith, a street contractor from Detroit, was very much put out. He said this was the first time he had ever failed in an undertaking, and he hated to go back home and say he failed in this. They worked several summer months and left. About ten days later, Mr. Smith returned with a Norfolk diver and his small schooner, and worked (or pretended to work) on the wreck. He remained aboard the schooner, though all the others roomed on shore. He probably remained ten days and then returned to Norfolk, where he reported he had gotten up a safe and that there had rusted in it a small hole, through which some gold coin had dropped out when he hoisted it on deck. He said that he would not break it open till his company ordered it.

I never knew what was done with the safe, and it was never reported, as far as I know, that any gold was taken from it. I surmise that in order not to have to go back home and say he failed, Mr. Smith went to the expense of hiring a boat and diver and buying an old safe which had perhaps rusted in water, and anchored it over the *Cumberland* and had the safe lowered and then brought on deck as if it had been on the *Cumberland*.

The next season Mr. Smith sent his son down, and he hired the diver, West, and got up what he could of copper bolts and plates. This company no doubt still owns the boat, but when they began dredging around the wharves, the government allowed the mud to be dumped into this hole in the channel, and no doubt now the boat is entirely covered over with mud. It was quite a unique pleasure, and often enjoyed, to take out parties of young people visiting us to see the diver go down and come up, and to feel the shock of the torpedoes he would explode, and see the water boiling all around us. The charges were seldom larger than 25 pounds of powder, and in this deep water the surface water was thrown up but a very few feet.

West was very superstitious, and if the charge did not go off or did not blow the boat to pieces as he expected, and we had any ladies on board, he would declare it was because they were there. But generally he liked to have us come to see him. He was, when I first saw him, a splendid-looking fellow, who must have measured over six feet and weighed over 200 pounds, but this deepwater diving injured his health, and he reduced rapidly and did not live long.

After I gave Mr. Huntington ten acres of my twenty on the river, with the express understanding he was not to condemn the other, yet in every way he tried to get the other or to make it so disagreeable to me that I would sell out. He did not contest the right to the property of those who sold to him, but paid the amount to them. He was not satisfied with the title he received from the purchasers of the Newport News farm (West's), so [he] sent a lawyer, James H. Storrs, down to secure the right from father's heirs, of the property he had bought. After getting this right and thus a clear title, he did not seem to care that he had to pay for our right or wish to enter suit against those from whom he had purchased. In fact, his contract with us was such he could not gain much by going into a lawsuit with them. But the fact that he did not sue did not prevent our suing for the parcels of the farm that we had not surrendered our right to. We had hoped he would sue and save us the expense, as a decision in his favor would have been also in ours.

Burroughs brothers of Norfolk agreed to take our case if we would give them, in case of gaining suit, the five acres of Mrs. Groome, and if also [we were willing] to bear one-half of all expenses of the suit. They failed in the lower and [Virginia] Supreme Court, as we had waited so long and until the property was valuable before making the claim. They then decided to get the case into the U.S. Supreme Court and had nearly succeeded in so doing when a decision of this court in a case in another state convinced them that it would be useless to go any further. By some complications, they had gotten the titles in—I have forgotten what they were—but they were able to get a few hundred dollars to clear it up. So, I am glad to say they were not out-of-pocket much, but spent a good deal of time on the case. It cost us about $400 each.

WILLIAM B. VEST, who came from Richmond in 1891 to help George Ben West organize the Citizens and Marine Bank, married West's niece, Bettie Bell Marrow.

George and Henry Schmelz of Hampton had organized Schmelz National Bank, a so-called private bank, in 1885. A month after George Ben West and associates organized their bank in 1891, a group headed by Theodore Livesey organized the rival First National Bank of Newport News. George West's bank drew heavily on locally born businessmen, while the First National was the bank of the Huntington interests: the C&O, the shipyard, and the Old Dominion Land Company. In 1932 the Citizens and Marine merged with the Jefferson Bank, and in 1962 the Citizens and Marine Bank became an affiliate of United Virginia Bankshares, Inc., of Richmond. The First National in 1962 merged with First and Merchants National Bank of Richmond. The Schmelz National Bank liquidated in 1932, and its building at Twenty-fifth and Washington Avenue was acquired by the merged Citizens and Marine-Jefferson Bank.

Lemuel Hoskins Sclater (1842–1899), who advised George Ben West to become a banker, was engaged in the drug and hardware businesses in Hampton until 1892. He was grandfather of General Sclater Montague, Hampton attorney.

An 1898 newspaper ad for Schmelz Brothers Bank ran in the Newport News **Daily Press.**

Major General Nelson A. Miles, USA, whom George Ben West called on at Old Point in 1866 in an effort to recover his father's land, was commander at Fort Monroe from May 22, 1865, to September 1866, when Jefferson Davis was imprisoned there. When Southerners protested the shackling of Davis, Miles was removed from command. He later distinguished himself as an Indian fighter and was commanding general of the Army before his retirement in 1903.

Captain Jerome Titlow, USA, who carried out the command to shackle Jefferson Davis, did not deserve the criticism which George Ben West and other Davis sympathizers heaped upon him. On March 28, 1891, Mrs. Davis wrote Titlow and concluded, "With kind regards, which my Husband always cherished to the end of his life for you."

The two Episcopal ministers whom George Ben West conveyed from Newport News to Old Point to visit Jefferson Davis were George Woodbridge, D.D., rector of Monumental Church in Richmond, and Otto Sievers Barten, rector of Christ Church in Norfolk.

Nat Gammel, who was one of George Ben West's Hampton friends, was stationed at a Confederate Signal Corps installation on the James in Isle of Wight County in the Civil War. He later kept a store on Hampton's South King Street and lived on Eaton Street, formerly called Hospital Street and, earlier, Locust Street.

The Confederate privateer, *Florida*, was commanded during part of the Civil War by Captain J. N. Maffit, who lived at Cedar Grove Farm, Warwick County. The house is still standing on Cedar Lane in

Amid other warships in the waterway, the USS Monitor *and the CSS* Virginia *(formerly* Merrimack*) engage in ironclad battle.*

Newport News. The *Florida* was seized by the USS *Wachusett* at Bahia, (now Salvador) Brazil, in 1864, and brought to Newport News. There she was mysteriously sunk.

Efforts to raise $40,000 in gold thought to have been lost in the sinking of the USS *Cumberland* in the James River in 1862 were never successful. However, the iron anchor chain of the *Cumberland* was brought up in 1909 and is displayed at the Confederate Museum in Richmond. West's account of the finding of the chain and anchor of the *Congress* is actually that of the *Cumberland*.

The site of the battle of the ironclads *Monitor* and *Virginia* (formerly *Merrimac)* was close to Middle Ground light, about a mile and a half southeast of Newport News Point (site of C&O coal-dumping piers). The *Virginia* tried to destroy the USS *Minnesota*, which had run aground in the north channel of Hampton Roads, but she could not get close enough because the tide was ebbing. Returning the next day, March 9, 1862, the *Virginia* found the *Monitor* standing by. The sea battle followed.

George Ben West developed a dislike for Collis Huntington after Huntington acquired land for the C&O in 1880. Fulfilling his dead father's earlier promise to give ten acres of Newport News farm to anyone who would bring a railway there, George Ben West deeded ten acres of his inheritance to the C&O. He was offended that Huntington continued his efforts to obtain the other acres.

James H. Storrs of Brooklyn, was attorney for Collis Huntington and an incorporator in 1880 of the Old Dominion Land Company, with Huntington as president.

George Ben West and his sisters brought suit in 1886 to recover portions of Newport News farm which had been sold off in the 1870s to satisfy judgments against the Parker West estate. The case had been docketed in the United States Supreme Court when a decision in a similar case convinced the Wests' counsel their case would be decided against them. The Wests thereupon dropped the suit.

CHAPTER XV

Land and a School

FATHER, WHEN HE BOUGHT THE NEWPORT NEWS farm about 1831, or at least a few years after, had an idea that it would be at some time a city on account of its fine harbor. Almost from my earliest recollections I had heard him so prophesy, and his neighbors and friends often tried to tease him about it, but he took all their jests about it in good humor and never lost faith. Vessels in those days were very much smaller than now. There were no three-masted schooners (for I can remember when they were first built), and I suppose the largest would carry not over 150 tons. Being so small, they required in the northeastern storms a good harbor and good anchorage. So instead of anchoring as now in Hampton Roads, they came in front of his, the Burk and the Wilbern farms and very close inshore. Often there were 100 or 200 so anchored.

About 1858, when the [U.S. Army] Ordnance Shops were put up at Old Point, Mr. John S. Millson, Congressman, tried to have them built at Newport News. Had they been built here, we would have had a village here before the war.

The captains of these [produce] boats either owned or had an interest in them, and the mates were either their sons or of some of the owners, and the crew was made up of their friends or neighbors, so the sailors were of much better class than we find at this time.

The Pumpkin Hall tract father bought from the Mourings, the grandfather of T. R. Mouring, and we always called the place "Mouring" or "Mouring's". I never heard of the name "Pumpkin Hall" till after the war, though I suppose it was so named because of the fine pumpkins raised by old man Mouring. Grandfather, father, and son were all good farmers and highly respected as reliable, good men.

I have mentioned that I was naturally lazy. I have always been fat, and on my 18th birthday I weighed 198 pounds. This was perhaps one cause of my laziness, and then I never was required to do any work but always called on servants to wait on me. And so, with my indolent habits, my liver was often torpid, and in '55 in the spring, I was quite sick and the doctor advised father to send me on the farm, and [me] to walk to school—about one and a half miles. I went to Mr. Crawford's, whom I have spoken of as dying at our house with yellow fever.

During and after the war I had to stir to help the family. I will record how I got the reputation of being very industrious. It was about '74 or '75, and I had a patch of peanuts that required working, and I could not hire a negro that day. It was fearfully hot, and after dinner I hitched a horse to a cultivator, the first time I had ever used one, and it was hard work. Mr. Pompey Marrow, commissioner of revenue, passed and saw me, and he told everyone he met how industrious I was. I finished in a few hours and went home to lie down. (He did not know this.)

In 1890 my sister, Mrs. Marrow, and I sold our portion of the Casey farm, inherited from our father, to the Newport News Land and Development Co. I took 100 shares in this company. Just after, Dr. A. E. Dickinson purchased a portion of the Ivy tract, adjoining our tract, and formed the Central Land Company. Col. Carter M. Braxton was the president of both companies. Either the colonel or the doctor conceived the idea of establishing here an academy to belong to the Baptists. No doubt the idea was to advance the value of their lands. It was perhaps Dr. Dickinson who brought the matter to the attention of the directors of the Old Dominion Land Company, who owned nearly all the land in this section, and at one of their meetings in '91 or '92 they passed a resolution to give to the academy a block in the city on which to erect the building.

Mr. C. B. Orcutt, Dr. A. E. Dickinson, Colonel Carter Braxton, and I selected Block No. 237. The conditions were that the Baptists should make their contribution at least $50,000 for building, etc. Dr. Dickinson had some years before been very successful in raising money for Richmond College, particularly at the North, and was by long odds the best canvasser among the Baptists. The Old Dominion Land Company directors thought no doubt he could easily get this amount from the 125,000 Baptists of the State.

Richmond College, under its charter, could receive money or land in any county, to found or maintain academies, and knowing this and after consulting with Dr. C. H. Ryland, in whom I have the most profound admiration and uttermost confidence for his wisdom and judgment, I agreed to give the 100 shares of the Newport News Land and Development Company stock to the college to establish the academy here. E. T. Ivy promised some stock he held in the Central Land Co. Dr. Dickinson and Colonel Braxton agreed to give also liberally to it. I don't remember that they promised anything specific, but the impression was left on my mind that they, as well as others in the companies, would help and that to a considerable amount. The stock of the Land and Development Co. was then estimated to be worth about $200 a share, the Central Company stock about $50, I think. This valuation was based on the estimated value of the lots, which had averaged about $200 each at public sales.

About this time the Land and Development Company offered to sell to their stockholders lots at their scheduled price for stock, valuing stock at $200 a share. I purchased one hundred lots with my 100 shares, the lots being selected by Colonel Braxton, M. B. Crowell, and I. I decided to have these lots deeded by the company direct to Richmond College, believing it to be better to have them managed by the trustees of the college than by local trustees, as it would be more certain to be under Baptist control. The deed cited they were given by me for the purpose of maintaining and establishing a Baptist academy at Newport News.

Colonel Thomas Tabb, who drew the deed (not at my suggestion but rather under my protest) put in a clause as he said to protect me, in which the land and all monies on hand for the sale of the lots would revert to me unless the academy was established by 1900. (I think this was the date.) Not intending to avail myself of this provision and not feeling it to be very important to start the school at once, and wishing to get as high a price for the lots as possible, we did not put the lots up for sale but only sold when parties wished some particular lot and were willing to pay a good price for it. We did not have to pay any taxes on them, and the prospect was they would increase in value. Mr. Orcutt, who was a director in the Old Dominion Land Company, told me that the company would consider these lots as $20,000 of the $50,000 to be raised to secure the block his company

Richmond (Va.) College, from **Harper's Weekly** *of June 14, 1873.*

promised. None of the others gave anything, and as the matter of securing contributions from the Baptists in the state was not pushed as perhaps they thought it would and should be, the directors of the [Old Dominion] Land Company very soon rescinded their order to give us a block in the city.

Still, I was in hopes that even if the academy should start in a much less promising way it would grow and perhaps be of great benefit to the boys and girls of our city. And I hoped that in the future someone, and perhaps many, would aid it and thus [enable it to] become a large school, whose influence would be for the elevation of humanity and training the young in Christianity and the glorifying of God.

When the time was about to expire when the land and money would revert to me, we had not started the school. About twelve lots had been sold, and Dr. C. M. Ryland, Jr. of Richmond College had in hand about $3,000. Colonel Tabb wrote to me suggesting that I give up the idea of having an academy and that I donate this property to Richmond College, the income of which should be used in educating boys of Newport News at the College. Drs. Ryland and [Frederic W.] Boatwright both urged the same plan. They said Newport News had a good high school (free) which would teach such branches as we proposed at the academy, and unless the academy was endowed sufficiently to compete with the free schools, or offered some inducements not attainable in the high school, that it could not hold out very long and would eventually prove a failure. But, they said, the gift of land and money to the college for the education of the youth of Newport News would last as long as the college.

I had a great deal of confidence in the judgment and opinions of all three of these gentlemen. In fact, I know of none on whose advice I would more confidently rely, though I felt they were naturally biased on account of their connection with the college. I became a little doubtful whether I should go contrary to their advice, and lost somewhat my faith in the future of the academy.

I have never believed that the free school exerts the same influence for good over the minds and characters of the children that the private school does. The teachers of the public schools feel their responsibility more to the trustees than to the parent or child. They teach the mass and do not care to encourage and help the individual who may be dull, or encourage and push forward the one who is bright. They do not inform the parent of what is best for the child, either in the study of books or training in other matters. The parent throws the whole responsibility of training and management of the child to a teacher and one who has perhaps just left school and gets his or her position just to make a little money, and for no love or capability for teaching, and [who] at the first opportunity for bettering himself or herself gives up teaching. The parent neither inquires nor seems to care whether the child is learning or what books are being taught. They pay their school taxes, or someone else pays for them, and they seem glad to get rid of the care and responsibility of managing their children.

The teachers are selected not because of their fitness always, but because they are the friend or related to the trustees in some way. The child, seeing his parents' indifference or careless attitude as to its progress in books or manners, does not have the incentive to do his best as he should have, and will often be satisfied with doing as well as others, and not try to surpass. The child must more and more have less respect and love and reverence for his parents. [The individual] looks to the state to give him schooling and as the years go by will become more and more dependent and want the state to do everything for them. The changing of a child to a different teacher every year also causes the teacher to have less influence over him.

All is different in a private school. The teacher must study the children and bring out the best in each one. The parent pays out his money and wishes returns for it, and investigates into all things pertaining to the school, both as to teacher and child; he wants results both as to training and scholarship. The teacher knows unless he is giving satisfaction he cannot succeed. The teacher of the private school is more apt to be one who is gifted in teaching and loves it and expects to make it his life's work. His character and deportment are more closely investigated, and he is apt to be more careful as to his acts and behavior.

The child, seeing his parent interested in what he is studying and how he is progressing, will naturally do better work, and will love his parents better, seeing them take an interest in his welfare. In denominational schools the teachers are selected as Christians, and who can tell the good a Christian teacher exerts over the lives of those they teach? How many children, even when very young, take their teachers as a pattern. And if so, how important to give them patterns which we would like for them to imitate.

The Catholics know the importance of having the young to teach. This also induced me in going contrary to the advice of my three friends, for the Catholics had established a school near Old Point, one between Newport News and Hampton, and one here [in Newport News]. They seemed determined to capture this section. This is Baptist ground, nearly every foot of it had belonged to Baptists, and I could not bear to think of these Baptist children so far forgetting the faith of their parents as to become Catholics without an effort on my part to counteract this influence.

Besides, if I acted on their suggestion, only a very few boys could take advantage of the college course, whereas the academy if successful would help a much greater number and, being under Baptist influence and its course of study being regulated by the college, would be the means of adding a much larger number of students to the college. And taking it religiously and denominationally, I thought there could be no comparison. The property having been my father's and he having such great faith in the city, though he had not lived even to see it commenced, my idea was to help the town more than the college. The future will determine what was best and who was right.

So I had another deed drawn, giving the property in fee for the establishment and maintenance of the academy, and it will have to be so used, as I first intended. On terms of a resolution of December 15, 1891, the trustees of Richmond College, in December 1893, accepted the gift and resolved that the financial secretary take such steps as will judiciously enlarge this gift by soliciting further subscriptions. Drs. Ryland and Boatwright a few years after this tried to get a donation— or at least a lease—from the Old Dominion Land Company, and also from Mrs. [Collis P.] Huntington to put up a building for a school on some of their vacant property near the river south of the shipyard, but did not succeed. I think nothing more was done until 1902, when Dr. Boatwright saw Mr. I. E. Gates about the Huntington school block, asking him to see the legatees of Mr. Huntington's estate to get them to give the block with the understanding that the academy would introduce an industrial feature in its course. There was no formal answer to this request from Mrs. Huntington or her nephew [Henry E. Huntington].

Mrs. Collis P. Huntington, later Mrs. Henry E. Huntington.

E. T. Ivy lost his stock in the Central Land Company. That is, it became worthless, and he has not been in a position since to give anything, though I still hope that he may give us something. Dr. Dickinson, by the sale of lots and land bought from Ivy and sold to the Central Land Company, made perhaps as much as $50,000, yet he has not, nor do I expect him to, given anything. He not only invested quite largely in land here, but also in many places in the state, and though he made money here, he lost in almost all the other places where he invested, so I am not sure that he made anything by his speculations, though I think he did. I am confident that he took and is still taking a great interest in the academy and wishes it success for the good he thinks it will do. Still, the impression was made, though I think an injustice was done him, that he talked and wrote about the school to increase the value of his property here.

I feel sure that the directors of the Old Dominion Land Company thought so, and with them he may have injured the prospects of the school. I think it more than probable they had the same idea as to me, particularly as the conditions in the first deed were that the property should revert to me after so many years, and we did not seem anxious to make sales or seem to be in any hurry to start the school. I never in the slightest degree intimated that I wished them to help us, and my only idea and desire has been the good of the youth of the city and not the slightest hope or wish for the increase of values of my own property or to benefit myself in the least degree. The action of the State Convention [of 1901–2] in taxing lands held by schools unless actually used and occupied for school purposes has made it somewhat necessary for us to sell the lots we now own when we can get even a fair price, rather than hold them to increase in value.

Before this action of the Convention I had determined to give some more land to the academy and wrote to Dr. Ryland to know if there was a limit to the holdings of Richmond College of land for academies. Also, how the trustees proposed to govern the academies, whether by local boards or by themselves. He wrote there was no limit as to the amount of land they could hold for the academies, but before I made up my mind what land to give, the Convention decided on the taxes. As the land was unimproved and would therefore be an expense to the fund till it could be sold and there was no demand at that time for such land, I concluded not to give it. Dr. Ryland wrote that the trustees [of Richmond College] had never considered the question of how the schools founded under its charter should be governed, but the matter had been spoken of and he thought there would be entire agreement to have a local board.

At the semi-annual meeting in 1902, Dr. Ryland introduced a resolution that a committee be appointed to confer with me about this matter. Drs. William E. Hatcher, Charles H. Ryland, and Frederic W. Boatwright were appointed. Dr. Ryland wrote out a report of the committee and sent it to me to examine and correct if necessary. In April this committee came down here [to Newport News] and talked over the matter and went over the report submitted, made corrections and then adopted it just as it was passed by the trustees in their annual meeting in June 1902. The report was adopted after a prolonged and critical discussion, and this debate developed the fact that, in the opinion of most of the members, the school would be of great help to the town as well as to the college.

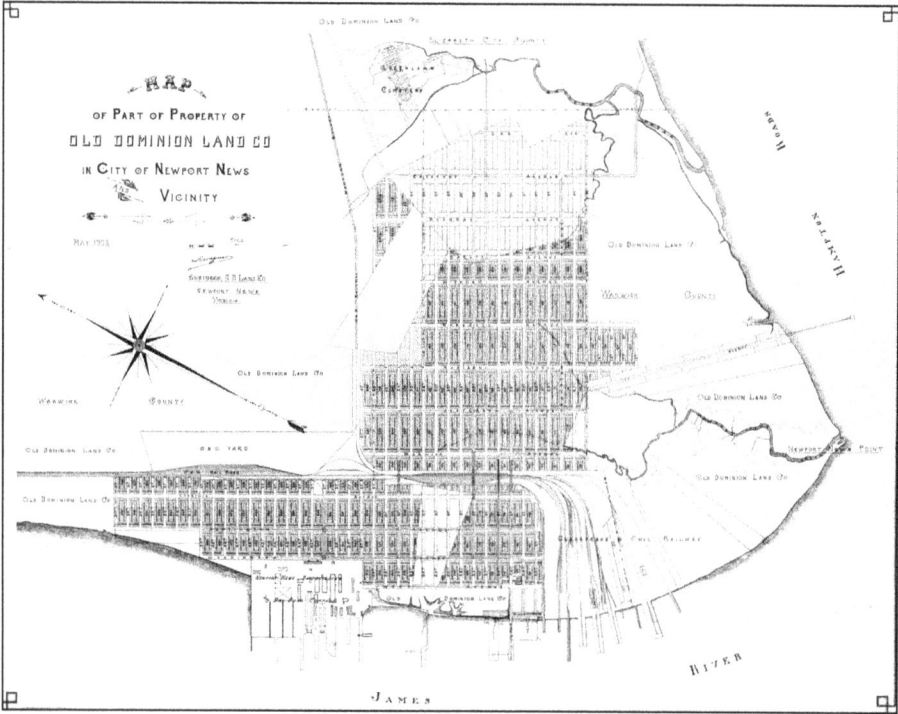

1903 plat map of the Old Dominion Land Company, showing the extent of its industrial and residential development at Newport News Point.

CONGRESSMAN JOHN S. MILLSON of Norfolk, who represented the First Virginia District in Congress from 1849 to 1861, proposed to the War Department that Army ordnance shops to manufacture and repair cannon be built in Newport News. The shops were built instead in 1858 at Fort Monroe.

The Pumpkin Hall tract, or Mouring's, which Parker West added to his Newport News farm, was a 60-acre property extending from Thirteenth to Twentieth streets and from Terminal to Madison avenues. Its value was enhanced by the C&O Railway right-of-way nearby.

Pompey Marrow was commissioner of revenue of Warwick County. His 600-acre farm was on the present Harpersville Road in Newport News.

Colonel Carter M. Braxton, CSA, was a civil engineer who surveyed for the C&O railway from Newport News to Lee Hall. He laid out much of early Newport News, and supervised excavations for the shipyard. He was vice president of the First National Bank when organized in 1891 and president of the street railway system of Newport News and Hampton.

Calvin B. Orcutt, formerly of Elizabeth, N. J., was first president of Newport News Light and Water Company, chartered in 1889. He became president of the shipyard in 1889. Orcutt Avenue was named for him.

The Rev. Charles Hill Ryland, D. D. (1846-1914) devoted most of his life to the University of Richmond. At the time he came to Newport News in hopes of establishing a private academy, he was simultaneously librarian, treasurer, and trustee of Richmond College, which became the University of Richmond in 1921.

M. B. Crowell was a post-Civil War postmaster of Newport News, an agent for the Old Dominion Steamship Company, and an Eighteenth Street storekeeper. He later moved his store to Twenty-third Street and West Avenue.

Frederic W. Boatwright (1868-1951), who counselled George Ben West in his efforts to create a Newport News academy, was then president and professor of modern languages of Richmond College. He retired in 1946 and served as chancellor of the University of

Richmond until his death in 1951.

Early Catholic parochial schools were established in Phoebus, on LaSalle Avenue in Hampton, and on Thirty-third Street in Newport News.

Isaac E. Gates, whom the Baptists besought to give Huntington-owned land for an academy, was an incorporator and treasurer of the Old Dominion Land Company in 1880 and was a brother-in-law of Collis Huntington.

When Collis Huntington died August 13, 1900, he left an estate estimated at $150,000,000, divided chiefly between his wife Arabella Yarrington Huntington, his stepson Archer Huntington, and his favorite nephew and associate, Henry Edwards Huntington. His widow later married Henry Huntington.

The Rev. William E. Hatcher (1834-1912), who served with Drs. Boatwright and Ryland on a committee to consider organization of private academies in Virginia and their relation to Richmond College, was a trustee of the college from 1870 to 1912. He was the college financial agent from 1901 to 1906.

Newport News Shipbuilding

Collis Huntington made Newport News into a major industrial center before he died in 1900. Here he works at his desk with a view of his ship-yard behind him.

CHAPTER XVI

A Baptist Academy

WHILE THE [RICHMOND COLLEGE] COMMITTEE was here in April '02, it was decided to open a [private Newport News] school in September, and they looked over the town for a suitable location. They selected the house that had been used as an ice cream saloon on the Casino grounds, on account of its situation and fine playgrounds. We rented it for $20 a month from September 15 to June 15, 1903. At a called meeting of the trustees after their semi-annual meeting in February of 1902, it was also decided to open an academy in Richmond in one of the buildings owned by the college.

In the discussion on the subject, I was much encouraged by what they said of the assured success of such an academy, for though our city is not as large, yet their [Richmond] high school stands very high as a school to prepare pupils for college, and they were so well satisfied of the benefit and success, if established, that they were willing to lend to it funds to start it. They did not have a penny to start theirs with, whereas we did have a fund that would keep us going for some years.

It seemed to me we had as good right to expect success as they, though it might take a longer time to get ours on a paying basis. Dr. Ryland and Dr. Boatwright both advocated the starting of the Richmond Academy, and I do not know whether they have changed their views as to the school at this place. But I am satisfied they will do all in their power to advance its interest and make it successful.

The committee decided to have two teachers, and Dr. Boatwright selected E. S. Ligon and Goodwin Frazer. Ligon, the principal, had several years' experience as teacher and expects to make teaching his life work. At the annual meeting in 1902, the trustees, after adopting the report of the committee, on my recommendation, appointed

W. E. Barrett, Maryus Jones, George F. Adams, and Dr. Thomas J. Sims on the local board, as well as H. L. Schmelz and myself from the trustees, and the president of the college. These seven composed the board for the first year. On June 18, 1902, Drs. Hatcher, Ryland, and Boatwright came here to inaugurate the local board and to gain the sympathy and cooperation of the Baptists of the city and of Hampton in the enterprise, and to launch this new enterprise and bring it to the notice of the Baptists.

The announcements of the meetings seemed to have been misunderstood, so we had at the First [Baptist] Church, with a few exceptions, only those who attended our regular prayer meetings; it was held on this night. Dr. Ryland, as secretary of the college, in a short speech presented a certified copy of the report adopted by the trustees on June 12. Maryus Jones, on behalf of the local board, received it in a very good address. Dr. Boatwright then gave a very fine address on education, what it is, and what it has done for the world. Dr. Hatcher then spoke on the nature and value of an academy as a foundation for a liberal education, and the advantages of such schools to the denomination if they should be scattered through the State. Also, the advantage to the cause of Christian education. Dr. Porter, who presided, gave a very good talk at the beginning of the exercises. The next day the board met at the Citizens and Marine Bank, all being present except Mr. Schmelz, who was in Savannah. Drs. Hatcher and Ryland being present, they were given the privilege to make such suggestions as they should think proper and to discuss all questions brought before the meeting. The board was organized by the election of George B. West, president; Maryus Jones, secretary; W. E. Barrett, treasurer; and H. L. Schmelz, auditor.

Professor Ligon accepted the position offered but had made arrangements to go to the Chicago University during the summer to take a special course of study, so that it was decided to get his assistant as soon as elected to come here and canvass for the school during August. Dr. Boatwright, who was authorized to select and employ the assistant teacher, found great difficulty in securing the right man, and when he had secured Professor Frazer, it was impossible for him to come and canvass for the school.

When Professor Ligon left Chicago and came down [to begin teaching], nearly everyone had made arrangements for their boys (the board decided to admit only boys the first year), so at the opening of the school, there were only eight or nine scholars. The board then decided to let the Baptist pastors of the city and vicinity select ten deserving boys and give them free tuition for the first year. We in a few days got the ten boys. Then the board decided to admit girls if as many as six could be secured, but we had put it off rather late, and in February they decided to admit girls (and one did matriculate) and more boys were admitted during the session.

In writing about the gift of the Old Dominion Land Company of the block of land to the academy and giving the reasons I thought they had for withdrawing it, I ought to have said, for I believe it, that though they may have thought that I and Dr. Dickinson and others may have been influenced by a desire to advance the price of our properties, that there is no doubt that the *only motive* they had was to increase the values of their lands. And, that by selecting the block we did, their lands would have advanced in value a great deal more than any of ours, as we had no land anywhere near the location we selected. The fact that they rescinded their action when they thought the school would not be as great and valuable as they at first believed and expected showed that this was their only motive, and they did not donate to benefit the city but only themselves.

The houses we have rented from them they have charged us the highest rents for. Though they knew we were not only not making anything but must draw from our fund, yet though they were not using the house we rented and could not rent it for any purpose, yet they charged the school $20 a month for it. And the third session, when we thought it best to enlarge by adding a primary department, they charged us $40 for a house they were only getting $8 a month for because they knew we were anxious to keep in the same location and could not get another house.

The policy of the Old Dominion Land Company has been to get all out of the town possible and to give nothing for anything. The churches of every denomination have had to pay as much for their land as any individual. As a company they have never helped a single church, either white or black, although other companies in the East End have donated land to build churches on. The churches help any city, as everyone knows, and though these lands cost this company only a few dollars per acre, the highest not over $300—and most of it about $150—yet they have allowed the people who have come here and who have enhanced their property [to] cramp themselves to build churches and schoolhouses, and have not helped them by donating an inch of land or a cent.

And even the hospital that the people are now sustaining is in a house of theirs for which we are paying $75 a month, though if not so occupied they could not get $50 for it. And the money for fitting up this house for a hospital—$2,000 or $3,000—came out of the pockets of the people. They get all they can and give nothing. I do not mean to say that there are not one or two in the company that do contribute something, but I doubt if there is another land company in this country, formed to build a city, that has done so little to help schools, churches, hospitals, and even manufacturers.

In 1903, George F. Adams moved from Newport News and took charge of the Chamberlin Hotel at Old Point, so in the June meeting, on my recommendation, W. M. Parker was elected on the board in his place.

During the session of 1907 and '08, I paid to the treasurer of the academy $800 to run the school and informed the trustees of Richmond College that I would advance enough for the session of 1908-09 to run the school, but unless they took some steps to secure money for the session of 1909–10, that we would have to close, as we could not sell the lots except at a very great sacrifice. I advanced $1,600 to the school that session, so they owed me about $2,400 advance money and $700 for taxes I paid. The school had run down in numbers, though the standard was kept up. It did not seem to be accomplishing the good that the large amount of money expended ought to do.

The trustees of Richmond College evidently thought that a school of this kind at this place was not necessary and that money could not be gotten from other sources to keep it going. So we decided to close and not to open the session of 1909–10.

Notes on Chapter XVI

THE CASINO, the first site of George Ben West's Newport News Baptist academy, was a park laid out by the Huntington interests about 1883. It adjoined the Warwick Hotel, which opened to the public that year fronting the James at Twenty-fourth Street. The Casino grounds extended from Twenty-fifth to Thirtieth streets along the James River. A large outdoor pavilion in the park was designed for lectures, balls, Chautauquas, and entertainments. Billy Sunday conducted a revival there in the 1920s, and rallies and speechmaking were frequent. The park is today largely covered by buildings, but a small open portion is preserved around a statue of Collis Huntington by Anna Hyatt Huntington, wife of his stepson Archer Huntington. It is designated as Christopher Newport Park.

West's Baptist academy opened in 1903 in a building located on the Casino grounds.

Professor E. S. Ligon, principal of early Newport News Baptist academy, and Goodwin Frazer, moved away from Newport News when the school was closed.

Trustees of Newport News Baptist academy chosen in 1902 were William E. Barrett, attorney; Maryus Jones, businessman; George F. Adams, manager of Hotel Warwick and later manager of Hotel Chamberlin at Old Point; Dr. Thomas J. Sims, physician; and Henry L. Schmelz, a Hamptonian and a founder of the Schmelz National Bank of Hampton and Newport News.

The first hospital in Newport News was created in 1903 at Lafayette (later Huntington) Avenue and Twenty-seventh Street, in a building which had been Lafayette House, a hotel. In 1906 Dr. Joseph T. Buxton opened a private hospital on the Boulevard, which later became Mary Immaculate Hospital. He had been chief surgeon at Lafayette Hospital.

William M. Parker, who succeeded George Adams on the board of the Baptist academy, was a principal owner of Parker and Spencer, a Newport News furniture store.

CHAPTER XVII

A Good and True Confederate

IN [CHAPTER 13] I RECORDED THE MANNER IN which I jotted down these recollections, and that was written in August of 1903, nearly three years ago. I commenced this book about 1899, and what I recorded in [Chapter 7] was written about 1900. I had no idea that what I then wrote might be questioned in some future time, for I could not be mistaken as to my recollection as to the occurrence, though I am not sure as to dates. But something has happened which might throw a doubt on what I have written in [Chapter 7] about getting a discharge from the [Confederate] local defense, so I will now record in more detail.

I never looked at the fact that I was a member of a company and regiment in the Local Defense Corps as amounting to anything as to my war record, and had it not been for mentioning the raids around Richmond, I should not have perhaps mentioned the fact that I did belong to a company. So little did it impress me that I did not even remember the company and regiment I was in. I think the reason I came to recollect the name of the colonel of the regiment was that Colonel McEnerney was so prominent in New Orleans during Reconstruction days and afterwards was governor of Louisiana. I am not sure even now that I was in the regiment he commanded.

In June 1894, Confederates of Newport News organized Magruder Camp and invited me to meet with them. But believing at that time the camps should be composed of only soldiers and sailors in the Confederate service (active service), I did not attend the first meeting when organized, but, as their records will show, was then elected a member and have been quite an active one ever since. I have taken part and intimately associated with the Lee Camp of Hampton, most of whose members have known me from childhood and know my record in the Confederate Quartermaster Department. They all have always and even now recognize me as a good and true Confederate, though I doubt but few know I was ever a member of the local defense.

I was notified of my election in the Magruder Camp and the next meeting I attended. As none of the members had known me before or during the war, I stated to them the reason I had not attended at the organization and that I had been only a clerk during the war, but throughout the war was in the [Confederate] government service. I did not even mention that I had been in the local defense and had been honorably discharged from all military duty, for the matter had escaped me. They declared that I was eligible, and as I have previously written, I have ever since taken an active part in all its meetings and enterprises.

I think the first time I thought about having been enlisted in the local defense was when some of the members wanted me to serve as commander of the camp. This was a few years after organization, and I had a long talk with one of the comrades, telling him my reasons for not having my name mentioned and that the officers at least should be those who were in active service. But, as the finances had gotten in bad shape, I agreed to accept the treasurer's office and have had it ever since.

Talking over with him my war record brought to my mind, I think, the fact that I had actually served in the local defense in Richmond. I did not then, nor do I now, remember a single private or officer in my company, nor the letter of the company. My impression is now that one company was formed from the Quartermaster, another the Commissary Department, and so on. The more I thought of the matter, the more I wanted to learn what company I was in, so as to show that I had been discharged. I wrote to the [Richmond] *Times-Dispatch* in reference to the time when the warehouses were guarded but could learn nothing. J. W. Friend had received through the War Department in Washington [a letter] recommending, I think, a promotion, and he advised me to write to Washington to see if I could get my record. So in March 1905 I wrote the following letter:

Gentlemen:
I was a clerk in the Quartermaster Department at Richmond, Va. during the war 1861-65. In 1864 I was enlisted in the local defense

Col. McEnerney Regiment. I have forgotten the company.

I write to find out the date of my enlistment and also discharge.

and received the following reply from the Military Secretary's Office of the War Department, Washington, D. C., dated March 23, 1905:

The records show that G. B. West was a private of Company E, 3d Battalion (subsequently designated 3d Regiment) Local Defense Troops, C.S.A. He enlisted May 20, 1863, at Richmond, Virginia. A roll dated August 27, 1864, the only one on which his name has been found, bears the remark, "absent without leave."

I was utterly surprised that I should be marked on the roll of August 27, 1864 "absent without leave." As I previously stated, I do not know whether it was in the year '63 or '64, though I think it was '64 that I performed the guard duty recorded and had a gun and accoutrements given me. I have no recollection of joining *twice*, and if I served as the records show for 15 months, I am sure I was never called on to perform any duties or to attend any drills, or anything else that might indicate that I belonged to any company.

In 1885, George Ben West joined the Magruder Camp of Confederate Veterans, gathering with men like these Texas veterans to attend local reunions.

As I have previously stated, as soon as the family got a house [in Richmond] and moved in, I got a position under Major Whitfield, about July 1, 1861, and was transferred from his office to Major Maynard's. I left Richmond at midnight April 2, 1865, on a wagon in Maynard's train to Greensboro, and left Greensboro sometime after Lee's surrender. During this time I never left the city [Richmond] except as mentioned before on a furlough in 1862, to see the family in Lynchburg, and again in the fall of 1863 for probably a week with the Signal Corps. I was always at the office during the seven days of the week unless sick, and I do not remember that I was sick enough not to go to the office for more than a day or two at a time except during the spell of typhoid fever in 1862.

I could at any time have been found at my office, either in 1861 at Bank and Tenth, or afterwards at Ninth and Main, so if I was "absent without leave," they did not try to find me for they knew I was in the Quartermaster Department, and I think I was in the company composed exclusively of clerks of this department. It seems to me that it was only neglect on the part of someone to mark on the roll that I had been discharged.

I have a very distant recollection about the discharge. As soon as I found out that I had to go on duty the third night of the same week, I thought it was an imposition, and perhaps spite on the part of someone, because up to this time I had been exempt from all duty of this character. I knew I could not do my duty at the office and sit up as much as was required, for I had been sick for two or more years with what the doctors called chronic diarrhea. So I told Major Maynard that unless he could get me off from duty in the local defense, I would join the army, for I felt pretty sure I would soon be either detailed from or discharged in the regular service. I remember him giving me a letter, which I doubt I read. He told me to give it to the captain and when he signed it, to go to the colonel and then to General G. W. C. Lee.

All of these three were a very short distance from the office, and when I returned with all of their endorsements he took it to the Secretary of War on Ninth and Bank. Whether he brought the letter (I suppose not, for it was probably filed) or a discharge, I do not know, but he told me to take it to Broad [Street] that evening and give it to the one in command, which I did. I also surrendered the gun, etc. at that same time. I suppose he kept the order or letter—whichever it was—and must have reported it, and this is why I am surprised that the roll wasn't marked "discharged" or "exempt."

If all the papers of the [Confederate] War Department had been saved it would no doubt be among them, but I knew a good many were burned on the night of April 2, 1865, for I saw them taken out of the homes and carried to the Capitol Square and burned. All the

Hampton soldiers knew I was in the department during *all the war*, and many now living know of my never having left the city of Richmond, or been away from the office except from sickness, and having lived in the same house all the time. I will mention a few now living that know what I have written here is the truth: James C. Causey, Captain W. J. Stores, W. P. Marrow, W. J. Hawkins, Fred Elliott, James M. Vaughan.

I yield to none in my devotion and allegiance to the Confederate cause. I was faithful in all the duties I had to perform, and though I often felt that others were undergoing dangers and hardships I ought to share, yet I feel sure that I was of more advantage to the Confederacy in the position I held than I would have been in the field, so I feel hurt that at some time someone may find this record of the War Department and say I shirked duty and left my command without a cause. I know the record is not right, but I know not how to correct or prove it wrong except to do as I have done—state the facts. No one who knows me intimately would for a moment doubt but that I have written the truth.

My father never took a very active part in politics, though if possible he never failed to vote. He was a Whig. Colonel John B. Cary, my teacher, always discouraged us boys from having much to do with politics, saying we had better while young apply ourselves to our studies. So perhaps these were the reasons I cared very little about attending conventions and political meetings. I had no ambition to hold office, and there was in this section no chance for a white man, unless he was a carpetbagger or a scalawag, for a great many years. And at this time it was as much as I could do to make a living for those depending on me.

About the year 1875, I think, for some reason the negroes had no candidate in my district for magistrate, and someone put my name on the ticket, and I was elected. But as the Judge [William Royall] Willis had the appointing of a man if I did not qualify, I refused the honor. In '92 or '93, Mr. T. M. Benson, who had made a most excellent supervisor for the county, for some reason resigned, and Judge Peek asked as a favor that I accept his unexpired term, which I did, hoping and expecting that Mr. Benson could be induced to be reelected.

At the election, a Mr. Hughes was put up by those not representing the taxpayers, and my friends so insisted on my running against him that I yielded and was elected. My administration was very unsatisfactory to me, as the other two supervisors seemed to always combine to carry any measure they wanted. I have never sought or wished any office since we have become a city but have refused all solicitations of my friends to accept any office. I have always felt that I would not be of advantage to the city in any capacity.

I had a Christian father, mother, and mammy who I am sure were always praying for me, and I loved to go to Sunday school and church, and yet I was nearly 48 years old before I united with the church. I had always wished to become a Christian and intended to, but I had my own notions about conversion. All who I heard speak of their conversion spoke of it as instantaneous, as giving them great joy and peace, and they felt not the least doubt but that they were accepted, redeemed, changed, and regenerated. In my mind the wonderful conversion of Paul overshadowed all the others in the Bible, and I thought mine ought to be similar, at least so manifest that I ought not to feel any doubts or misgivings. I could not see that just repenting and accepting Christ and going forward when the invitation was given could or did indicate a change of heart. I did not seem to realize that Andrew, Peter, James, and John and Matthew were as truly as converted as Paul.

The statement of Christ to Nicodemus was another stumbling block to me, "Ye must be born again," though He had explained that "The wind bloweth where it listeth, and thou hearest the sound thereof but cannot tell from whence it cometh or whither it goeth, so is everyone that is born of the Spirit." Yet I could not see that this was the gift of God. I did not realize that "Whosoever believeth that Jesus is the Christ, the Son of God, is born of God, and whosoever is born of God overcometh the world," and that "the victory that overcometh the world" is ever our faith.

So years passed, and though I wanted to be a Christian and unite with God's people, I was afraid I would make a mistake as I did not have the assurance of acceptance and of being born again.

After the war, a Sunday school was established in Newport News, and I taught a class of girls but often felt condemned in not practicing what I taught. I also was persuaded to take a class of boys to teach in the [interdenominational] Union Chapel, and often again did my conscience condemn me. All this time I was hoping to realize that I had a change of heart and feel that I was a child of God. In 1885, my sister Lizzie, who was a member of the Hampton Baptist Church, died, and I thought that if I had been taken instead of she that I would not have had any hope of eternal life, for I never believed that any works could save me or anyone. My only hope was in Christ's love and mercy, and that I must be regenerated. I could not think of a changed heart without my knowing it without any doubts.

The interdenominational Union Chapel was built by the Old Dominion Land Co. in 1881.

Now I determined to do all I could to find out and then act upon what faith I had. The devil again assailed me by suggesting that I was frightened and that if I made an open confession now that people would say I was scared into taking the step. So I waited and waited much longer than I had intended, and thus nearly a year passed.

Coming down from Richmond on the train in 1886, Dr. A. E. Dickinson took a seat by me. I had known the doctor some time, before and during the war. After the completion of the C&O he had taken a great interest in the Baptist cause here and secured help from the State Board after our [Union] Chapel was built. He always stopped at my house when here, and so I began to know him intimately and to love and admire him truly. We had scarcely gotten out of the city before he asked me why I had not united with the church. I unbosomed myself, relating all my doubts and fears, and we talked on this subject till we arrived here, he trying to show me my duty and I giving all the excuses I could think of. He said that he and others with whom he had conversed had no doubt that I had been regenerated though I could not tell the time.

I want here to say if Christians would, when opportunity occurs, talk to their unconverted friends, that perhaps many would come out on the Lord's side who are now groping in doubts and darkness. I believe Dr. Dickinson did more of this than anyone I ever met, and only eternity will reveal the good he has accomplished by such conversations. I promised him that I would talk with A. B. Rudd, the pastor, and if he thought I was converted and would advise me to join the church, that I would write him to come down the next Sunday and baptize me, as he made the request to immerse me. I at once saw Brother Rudd and told him of the conversation and the promise. He agreeing with the doctor, I wrote and he came down and immersed me in the river in front of the bowling alley, opposite Twenty-Sixth Street. Brother Rudd also baptized some others at this time—October 3, 1886.

In the protracted meeting following, the Reverend C. W. Donaldson did the preaching, and the membership was about doubled and the members greatly encouraged. The church meetings had been held irregularly and no minutes recorded. The treasurer had not made a report for some time, and no one seemed to know how the church stood financially. Colonel Braxton, at one of the first business meetings, in nominating me for some committee after I had been given other work in his usual affable, pleasant, and jocular way, said that as I had not done any kind of church work for so long, that I ought now to do all the work possible. What he spoke in a sort of joke I took seriously and determined to do all in my power and not to shirk any work or position that the church placed upon me.

I have never regretted this but think it very fortunate that I was so determined, for after my baptism the devil again tempted me, saying "You have made a mistake in joining the church, you are not fit, you have not experienced the joy you expected in doing what you and others thought your duty," that I was no better and ought to have waited to be more certain I was accepted of the Lord.

My doubts and fears vanished by my resolve to do what I could, but not to trust in anything I did and only to believe that Christ would claim me as purchased by His blood, and trust only Him. If lost, I could not help it; I should be lost if He did not claim me, and I would rely on Him, and with His help try to do what the brethren thought I ought to do and seek to know His will, and with His help do it. I know how little I have done, and He knows how far short I have come in obeying Him and doing His will. I merit nothing, but as I am trusting that He will claim me as His, though so unworthy, and that He will take me to dwell with Him, that for such hope in His love and mercy, that I ought to do all I could to show my love of mankind and the glory of God. All things point that it has not had the divine approval, and if this is so I willingly give it up and submit to what seems to be the divine leading. May I not have misinterpreted providence. If I have, may God so rule that it may be for His glory.

Dr. Charles H. Ryland, secretary and treasurer of Richmond College, in sending me the deeds for the lots in the city and in Warwick County today, June 9 [1906], wrote:

> Please find the deeds enclosed. I hope they will prove satisfactory. The signing and sealing makes me sigh because of the disappointment. You and I had high hopes one time. But it becomes more and more clear every day that the *State* is going to press all private schools to the wall. We did not and could not anticipate this fact. Your intention was a noble one and has been most highly appreciated as disinterested and kind in every way.

Newport News Shipbuilding

Newport News was growing fast when the shipyard opened its first drydock in 1889 for the Navy monitor **Puritan.** *Collis Huntington arrived for the christening ceremony on his private rail car.*

THE CONFEDERATE Local Defense Corps, in which George Ben West had enlisted in 1862 in Richmond, served during the Seven Days' Battles around Richmond. Its commander was General George Washington Custis Lee, son of Robert E. Lee. West was in a regiment commanded by Colonel Samuel D. McEnerney, a native of Louisiana who later became United States senator and governor of Louisiana. He died in New Orleans in 1910.

The Confederate Secretary of War to whom General Custis Lee submitted George Ben West's discharge was James A. Seddon (1815–1880), a Virginian who lived at Sabot in Goochland County.

William Royall Willis was judge of Elizabeth City County Court from 1870-1881. The court, which existed from 1851 till 1904, had concurrent jurisdiction with Elizabeth City Circuit Court. He was father to John M. Willis, attorney, publisher of the Hampton weekly *Monitor*, and superintendent of Elizabeth City County schools.

Thomas M. Benson, whom West calls an "excellent supervisor" of Warwick County, had been engaged in Newport News since 1890 in the coal and supply company with Edwin Phillips. Benson-Phillips Company, Inc. continues to operate.

George M. Peek was judge of Elizabeth City County Court from 1886 to 1896. The court, which existed from 1851 to 1904, had concurrent jurisdiction with Elizabeth City Circuit Court.

Union Chapel, an interdenominational house of worship, was completed in 1881 near Twenty-second Street and West Avenue. It served all interested denominations until each built a church of its own. It was later used as the Sunday school of First Presbyterian Church on Twenty-Seventh Street and finally sold to Trinity Lutheran Church.

The Rev. August Bartow Rudd (1861–1944) was an early pastor of First Baptist Church of Newport News. After serving as missionary to Mexico and Puerto Rico, he retired in 1926 and was professor of bible at the University of Richmond until 1933.

The Farm that Became a City

IN 1906, GEORGE BEN WEST FINISHED PENNING THE story of his life. He had told all that he felt important—or all that his modesty permitted. He placed his memoirs among his family papers, where they were found on his death in 1917. Since that time the memoirs have been read and excerpted by several scholars, but until now they have never been published.

The interest of the memoirs lies chiefly in West's account of the Federal troops' seizure of his Newport News farm in 1861. However, they are secondarily useful as an inside view of the founding and early years of the city which Parker and George Ben West believed their farm would someday become.

Like most dreams which come true, George Ben West's Newport News was not the complete fulfillment he expected. The Yankee "drive" which motivated Collis Huntington and his minions was abrasive to the gentle, easygoing West. He was indignant at Huntington's seeming ingratitude for West's gift of ten acres to bring the Chesapeake and Ohio terminals to Newport News. He resented Huntington's efforts to acquire his remaining ten acres with the C&O trackage at Eighteenth Street. He thought Huntington's Old Dominion Land Company lacked community spirit and did too little to encourage churches.

It was Southern pride versus Northern aggressiveness all over again.

When Collis Huntington sent him a pass to ride the C&O, George Ben West returned it with a handwritten note of thanks. He could "afford to pay [his] own way," he wrote proudly.

After Huntington died in 1900, George Ben West continued to compete with "the Huntington interests". His Citizens and Marine

Bank vied for business with the First National Bank, and his real estate interests were often at odds with those of the Old Dominion Land Company. His closest friends were his aging Hampton and Newport News contemporaries in The Pioneers Club and in Magruder Camp of Confederate Veterans.

But his civic enthusiasm overrode any anti-Huntington feelings he may have had. The poor boy of Reconstruction days was by 1900 a wealthy man. He moved from a simple house at Seventeenth Street and River Road to his three-story Victorian mansion at Thirty-fourth Street and West Avenue, taking with him his sister, Missouri Smith, and her daughter and son-in-law, Mr. and Mrs. William E. Barrett. He was "the richest man in town," to some contemporaries. From his spacious West Avenue porch, he could look across his cannas and wrought-iron fence to the James River, alive with ships waiting for cargo or overhaul.

The Mariners' Museum

Collis Potter Huntington, left, who brought the C&O to the Peninsula, left much of his wealth and power to his nephew Henry E. Huntington, right, president of the shipyard. The name of the newsboy is not known.

Each morning he walked the six blocks to his bank. Arriving before opening time, he removed his coat and donned the black alpaca jacket which was his trademark. Seated in front of the vault doors, he transacted the days business with the aid of an all-male staff; women were too refined for commerce, he felt. He was a precise, thrifty, punctual businessman.

Quitting time at the Newport News Shipbuilding and Drydock Co., in downtown Newport News, about 1905. Huntington's vision for Newport News, as well as that of George Ben West, helped bring it back to prosperity after Reconstruction.

He was pleased when the *Encyclopedia of Virginia Biography*, edited by Lyon Gardiner Tyler, included him in its fifth volume in 1915, along with other leading Virginia men of the day. "Respected and admired for his material achievements," the account read, "Mr. West is held in high regard because of the sincerity and firmness with which he has remained true to principles of honor and uprightness in every department of life. His true worth is garbed in a manner of cordial friendliness, courtesy and consideration marking his every word and deed."

Though childless, he was concerned for the education and manners of future generations. Skeptical of public schools, he vainly tried to start an academy under religious auspices, hoping to duplicate the training he had received at John B. Cary's Hampton Academy of the 1840s and 50s. Failing that, he turned his hopes on Richmond

College, a Baptist institution which in 1921 became the University of Richmond. He served it as trustee, gave it many gifts, and saw his namesake and favorite kinsman, Benjamin West Tabb, become its treasurer and vice president.

As Mr. West grew old he judged the greatest need in Newport News to be better medical facilities. As a workingman's town, Newport News had few physicians or hospital rooms. The Newport News General Hospital had opened in 1903, but it had closed in three years when a fire killed five of its patients. Except for Dr. Joseph T. Buxton's excellent private hospital on the Boulevard (later to become Mary Immaculate), there were no hospital beds in the city of 20,000 people for several years after 1906.

To correct this, George Ben West in 1916 gave $10,000 to create Newport News General and Non-Sectarian Hospital—progenitor of today's community-sponsored Riverside Hospital. And because he saw especial need for hospital beds for the poor, he left the bulk of his estate on his death the next year for a charity hospital. This trust, amounting to nearly $1,000,000, was awarded by court decision in 1965 to Riverside Hospital to treat needy people in its outpatient clinic. On the wall of the Parker and Mary West Clinic there, a plaque reads:

In Grateful Memory of
George Benjamin West, 1839–1917
and Missouri Parker West Smith, 1841–1921
Founding and Pioneer Citizens of Newport News
By Whose Generosity and Love of their Fellowman
This Clinic was Made Possible
And in Grateful Recognition of the Untiring Efforts and Generosity of
Roderick Dunn Moore and his Wife, Virginia Tabb Moore
of Richmond, Virginia

It was a pleasant coincidence that his bequest to the city was paid in 1965—a hundred years exactly after Lee had surrendered and George Ben West had returned from the Civil War to Newport News. In that chaotic century, the place had more than achieved the growth Parker West had prophesied. True, Yankees were no longer hated in Newport News, for the lower Peninsula had become a melting-pot of North and South, of America and Europe, of army and civilian life. True also, the farms and forests which George Ben West had known as a boy on Newport News Point were all gone, together with many of the Southern folkways he had loved.

Most of the early roads were by 1965 hidden under concrete and macadam highways. Creeks of early Warwick and Elizabeth City counties had in many cases been dammed or filled. The counties themselves had been absorbed by the cities.

Yet something of the character of horse-and-buggy Virginia survived amid the noise and traffic of the new age. George Ben West's world had left its trace in a scattering of place names, farmhouses, roads, and legends. In its accent and its pace, the lower Peninsula was still clearly Southern. The ex-Confederate would have been pleased at that.

If America would know its past, it must preserve these remnants of those heroic early years. In a modest way, George Ben West's memoirs help us to do that.

BIBLIOGRAPHY

Brown, Alexander Crosby: *Chesapeake Landfalls.* Chesapeake, Va.: Norfolk County Historical Society of Chesapeake, 1974.

, editor: *Newport News' 325 Years: A Collection of Historical Articles.* Newport News: Golden Anniversary Corporation, 1946.

: *The Good Ships of Newport News.* Cambridge, Md.: Tidewater Publishers, 1976.

Chesnut, Mary Boykin: A *Diary from Dixie*, edited by Ben Ames Williams. Boston: Houghton-Mifflin, 1961.

Lavender, David: *The Great Persuader.* Garden City, N. Y.: Doubleday, 1970. Jester, Annie Lash: *Newport News, Virginia, 1607-1960.* Newport News: City of Newport News, 1961.

Myers, Robert Manson, ed.: *The Children of Pride: A True Story of Georgia and the Civil War.* New Haven: Yale University Press, 1976.

Rouse, Parke S., Jr.: *Cows on the Campus: Williamsburg in Bygone Years.* Richmond: The Dietz Press, 1972.

Stauffer, William Tilden: "The Old Farms Out of Which the City of Newport News Was Erected, with Some Account of the Families Which Dwelt Thereon," *William and Mary Quarterly*, v. 14, series 2, No. 3 (July 1934), pp. 203-215; no. 4 (October 1934), pp. 333-341; v. 15, series 2, no. 2 (April 1935), pp. 126-137; no. 3 (July 1935), pp. 250-266.

Starkey, Marion Lena: *The First Plantation; A History of Hampton and Elizabeth City County, Virginia, 1607-1887.* Hampton: Houston Printing and Publishing House, 1936.

Tyler, Lyon Gardiner: *History of Hampton and Elizabeth City County, Virginia.* Hampton: Board of Supervisors of Elizabeth City County, 1922.

, editor: *Encyclopedia of Virginia Biography*, 5 vols. New York: Lewis Historical Publishing Company, 1915.

Turner, Charles: *Chessie's Road.* Richmond: Garrett and Massie, 1956.

ACKNOWLEDGMENTS

AS EDITOR of the memoirs of George Benjamin West, I am greatly indebted to Mr. and Mrs. Roderick Dunn Moore of Richmond for permission to publish them.

I thank Mrs. Dorothy Stevick for kindly typing the manuscript, and Miss Lottie Driver, public librarian of Newport News, for assistance in obtaining illustrations, many of which were used by the Newport News Historical Committee in 1969 in its *Endless Harbor: the Story of Newport News*. Among the many friends and scholars who helped in various ways, I particularly thank Dr. Chester Bradley, Mrs. Sandidge Evans, the Right Reverend John Boyd Bentley, Mr. Thomas Chisman, Mr. E. M. Hutton, Mrs. W. Russell Winfrey, Jr., and Mr. Harold Sniffen, all of Hampton; Mr. Alexander Crosby Brown, Mr. Hairston Seawell, Mr. Charles Brooks, Mr. Roscoe Agnor, Miss M. Catharine Harrison, Mr. Robert Burgess, Mr. Sinclair Phillips, Mrs. Martha Ingles, and Mr. Thomas N. P. Cutler, and Mr. William Allaun, Jr., all of Newport News; Miss Josephine Nunnally, archivist of the University of Richmond; Miss Lottie Driver, city librarian of Newport News; Mr. Ardie Kelly, librarian of The Mariners' Museum; Dr. Louis Manarin, Virginia State Archivist, Richmond; and the staff of the Earl G. Swem Library of the College of William and Mary—particularly Mr. Robert Stevick and Mrs. Dortha Skelton.

To enhance readability, the editor has divided the memoir into chapters. Clarifying details have been inserted in the text within brackets, and further background is provided in notes following each chapter.

– *Parke Rouse, Williamsburg, 1977*

AS PUBLISHER of the second edition of George Benjamin West's memoirs, using all original manuscripts and only adding illustrations, I thank Wilford Kale for his immeasurable contributions of consultation, encouragement and writing. We intend this new edition not to celebrate the war, but only to be of interest to scholars and Virginians who want to investigate their own back story.

– *Marshall Rouse McClure, Norfolk, 2012*

INDEX